# ART

## FOR YOUR IMAGINATION

**B. Kornelsen**

Copyright © 2020 Beverley Kornelsen

All rights reserved. No part of this book may be reproduced, distributed, or transmitted in any manner whatsoever without the prior written permission of the publisher.

Publisher contact: BevKornel@gmail.com

KDP Print-on-demand edition

ISBN: 979-86448-317-4-6

# WHAT DO YOU SEE?

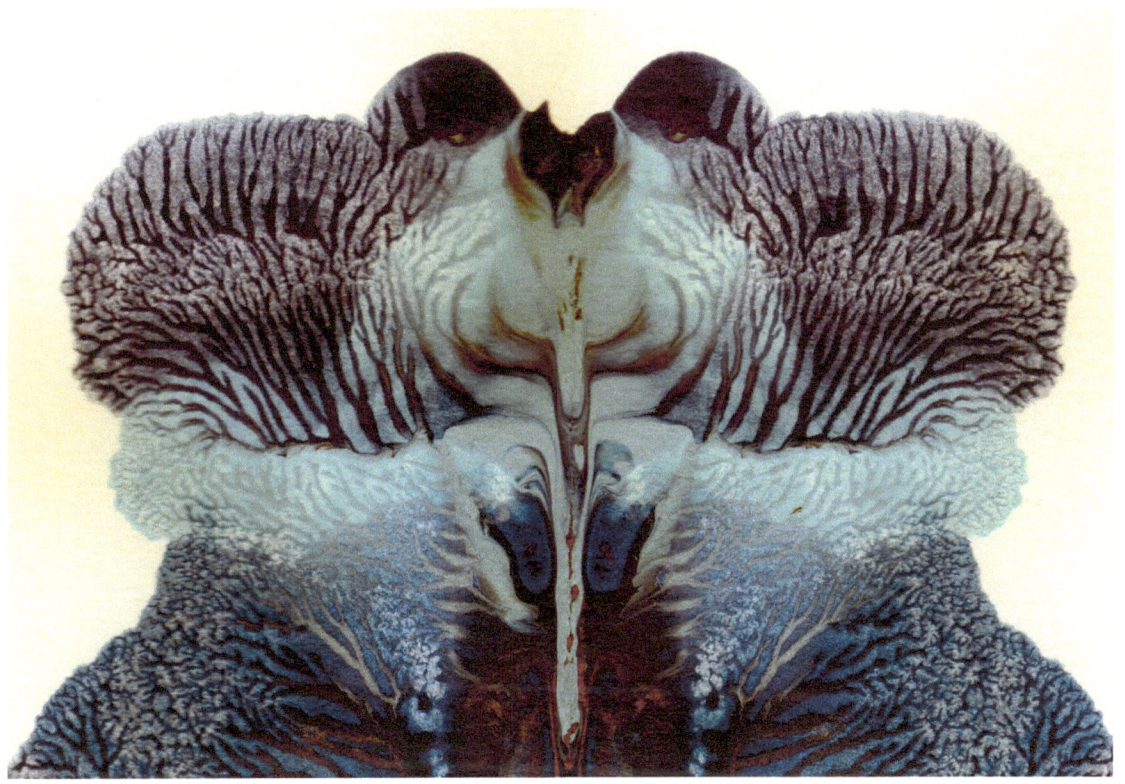

Image 1

To get the most enjoyment out of this book, don't rush. Go slow and really examine each image. Give your imagination lots of time to process what your eyes are taking in. Look not only at the whole, but the smaller details. Chances are, the more you look, the more you will see.

When I first looked at the image above, I saw a bear, albeit one with really wide cheeks. His eye sockets are protruding at the top of the picture and I can see the ruffles in his hair. Notice how calm he is looks.

When I look again with the image a bit further away, I can re-imagine it as an owl. Where I once saw the bear's cheeks, I can now see very small eyes on either side of a large beak. The owl looks as calm as the bear.

What do you see?

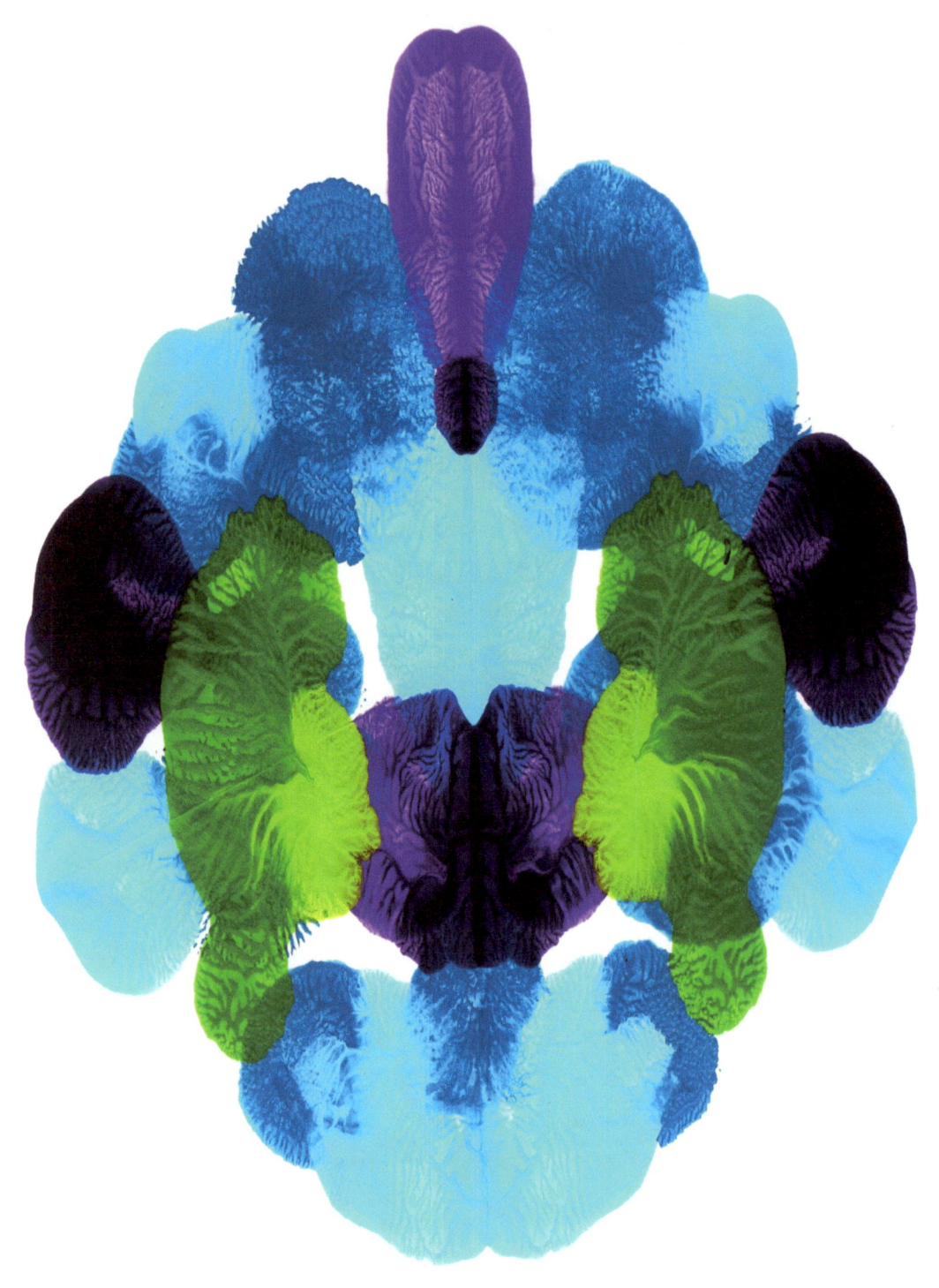

Image 2: A parrot or ?

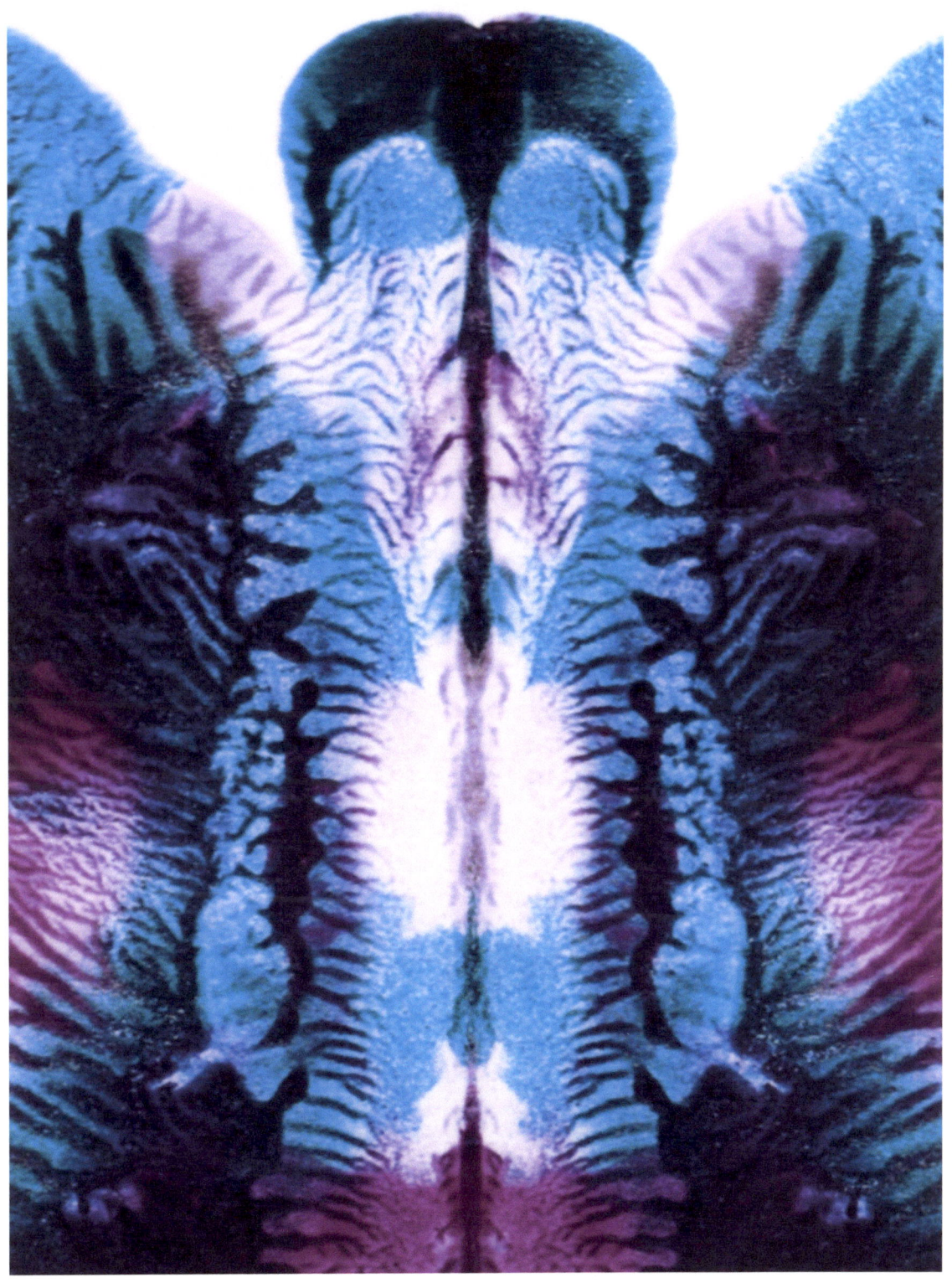

Image 3: A vampire, goat, or ?

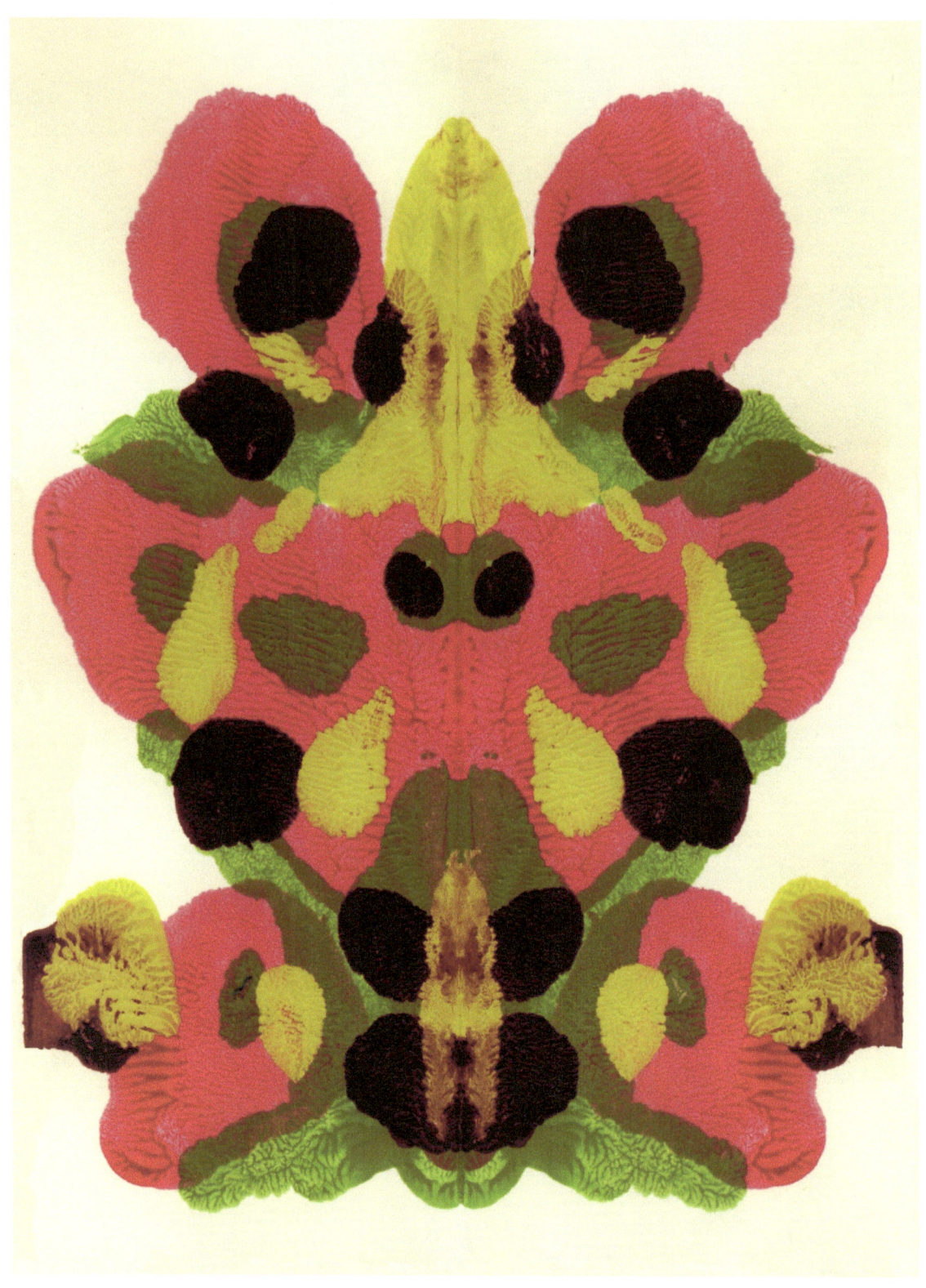

Image 4: A frog, rodent, or ?

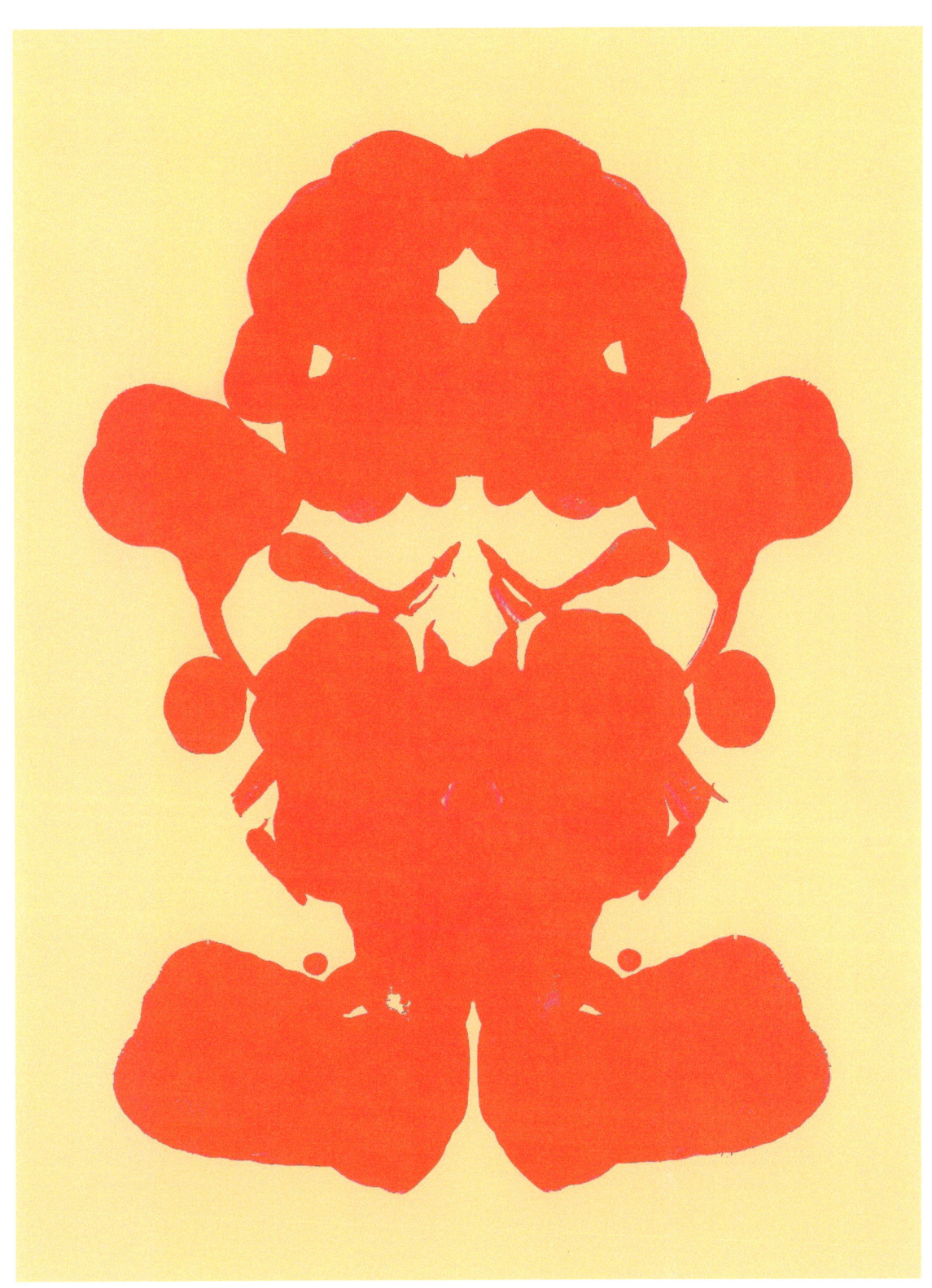

Image 5: A woman, amphibian, or ?

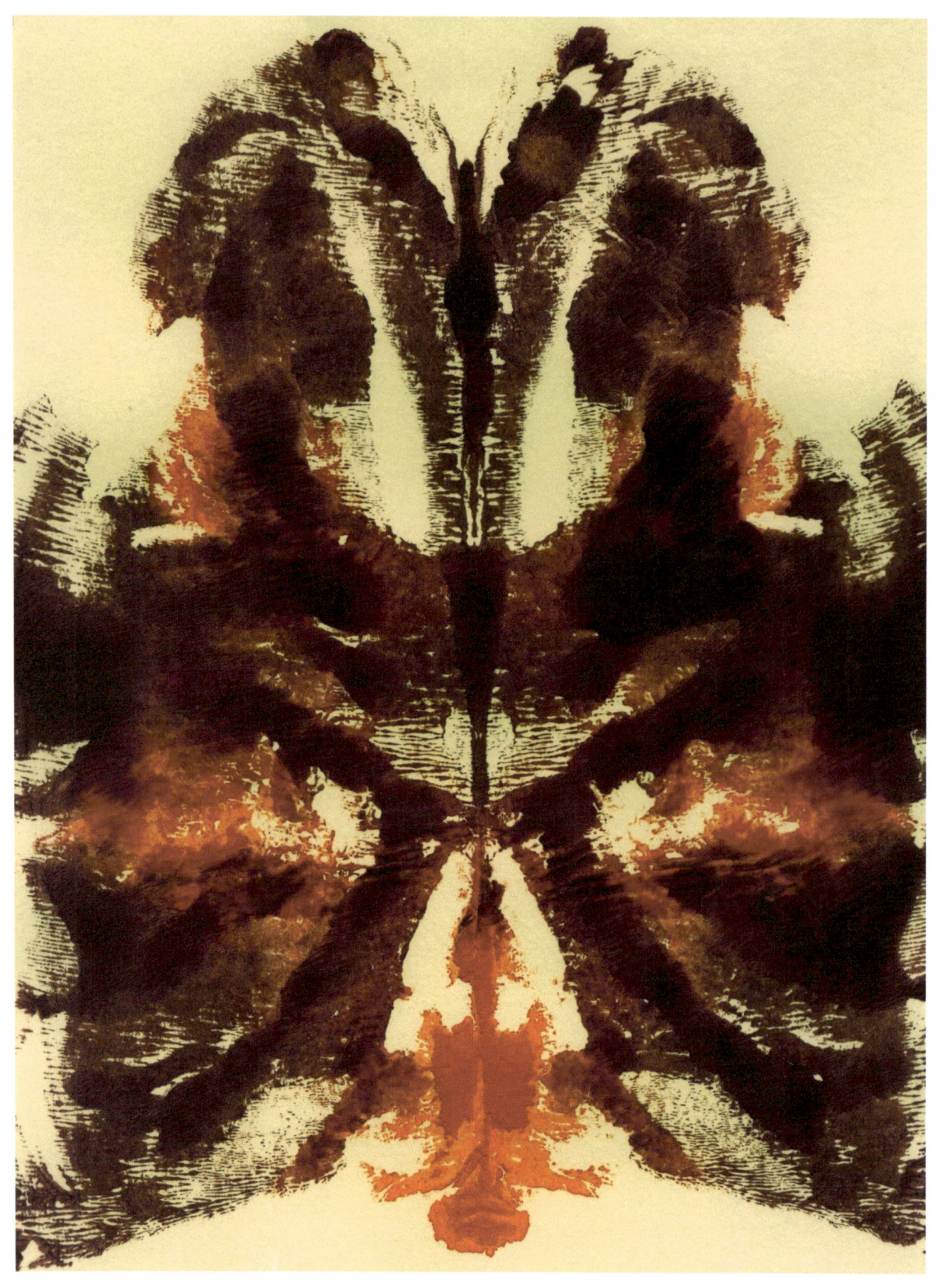

Image 6: A bird of prey, people, or ?

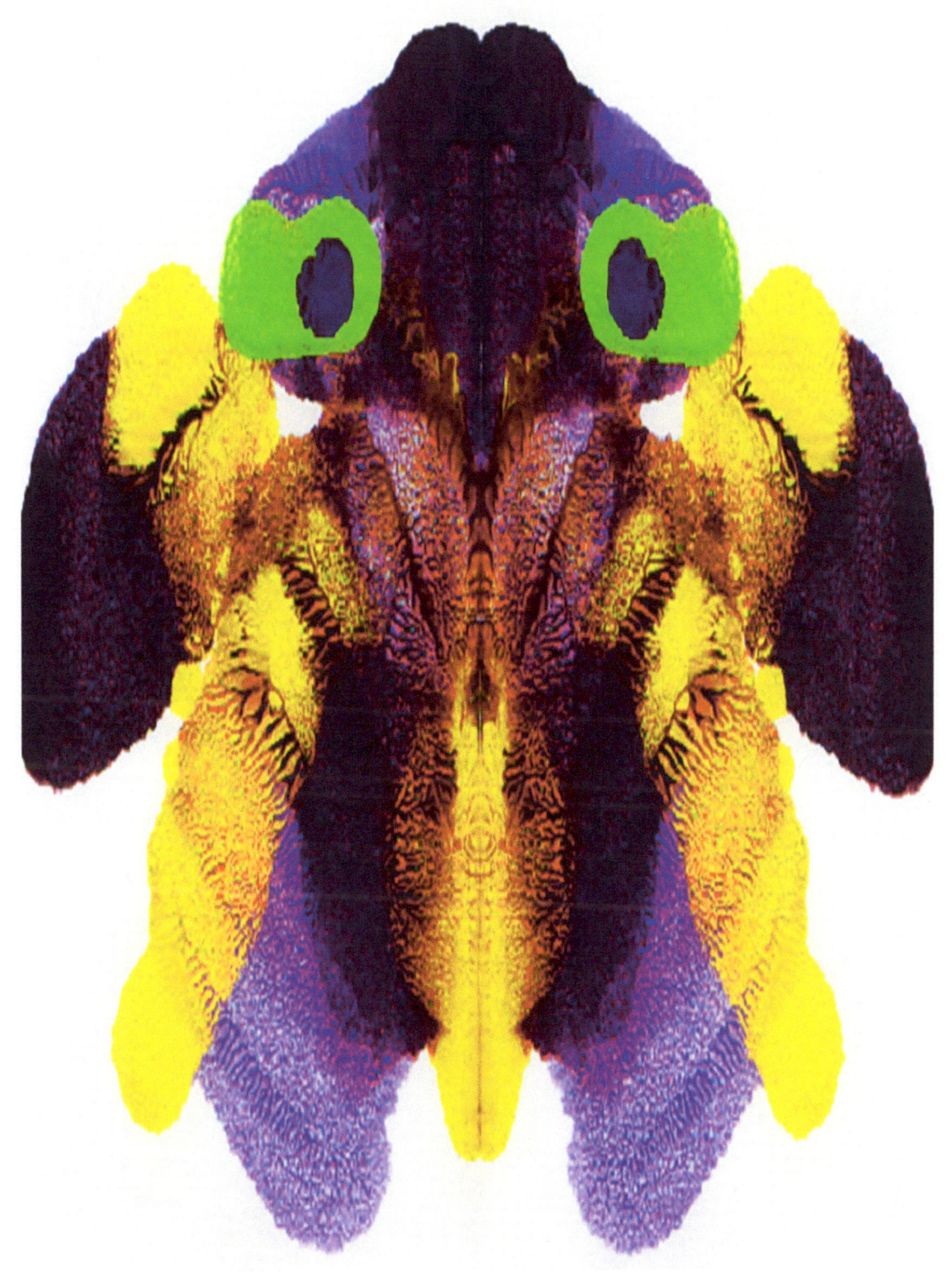

Image 7: A bee or ?

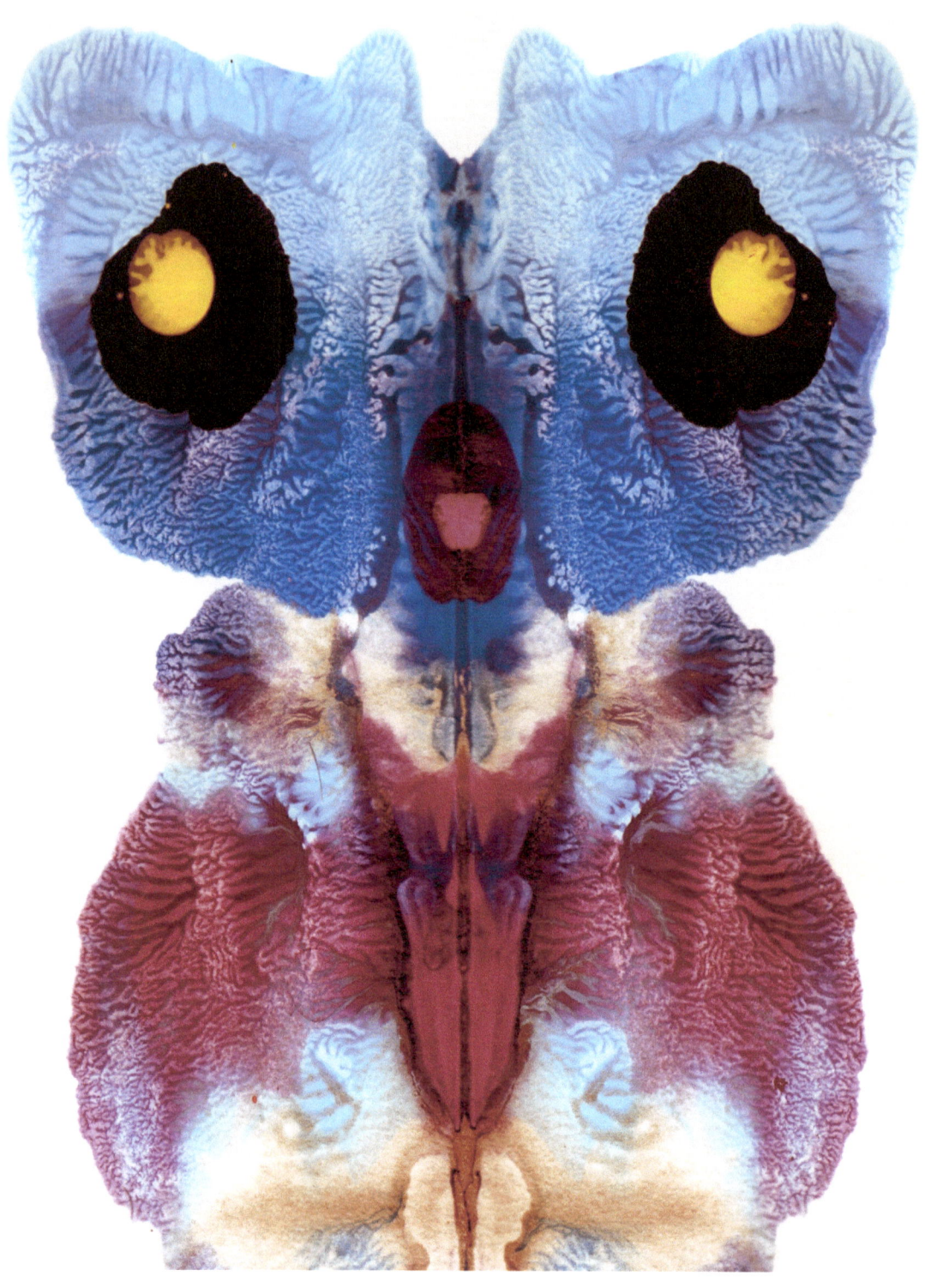

Image 8: An owl or ?

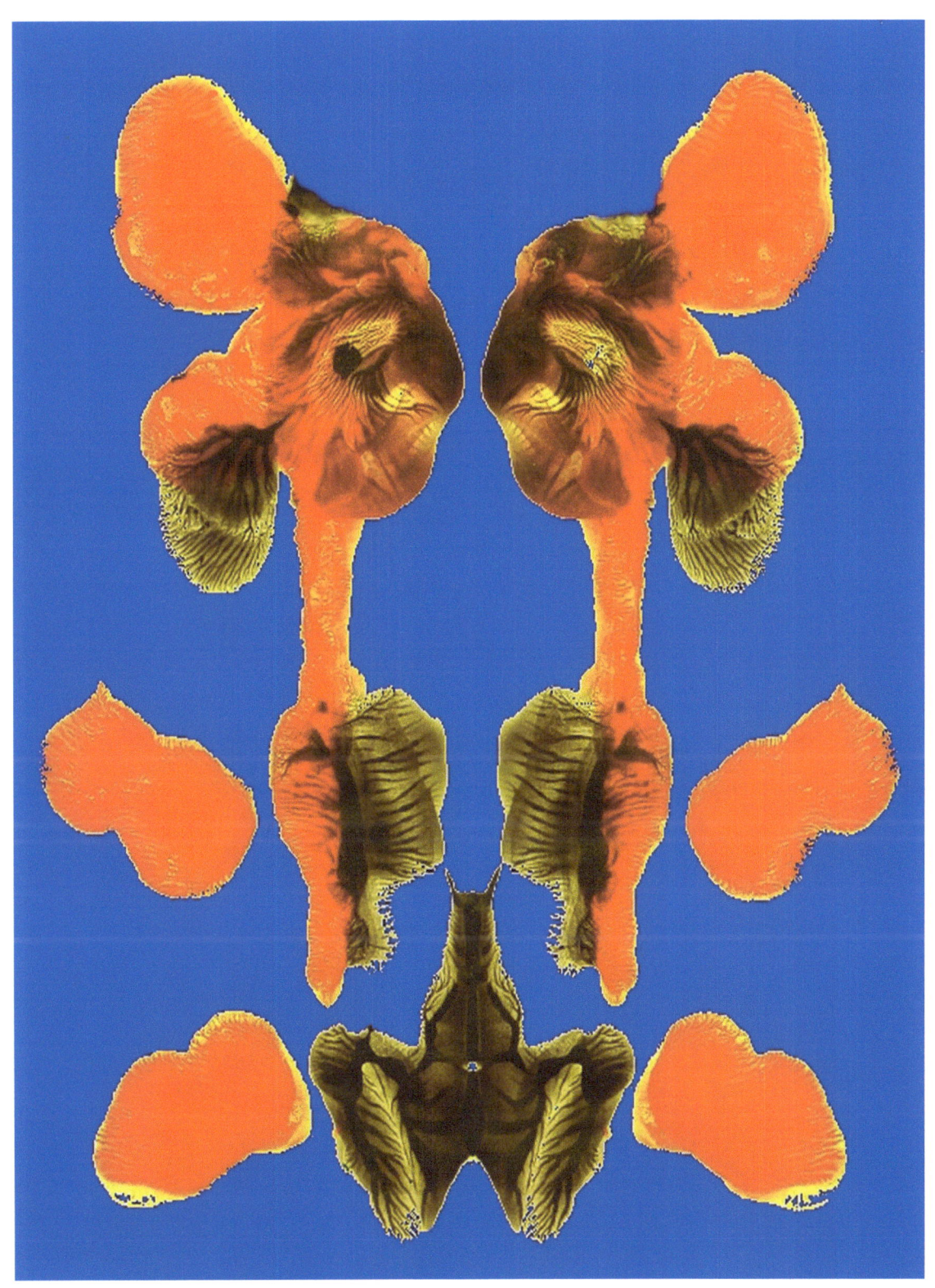

Image 9: Coy fish, rabbits, or ?

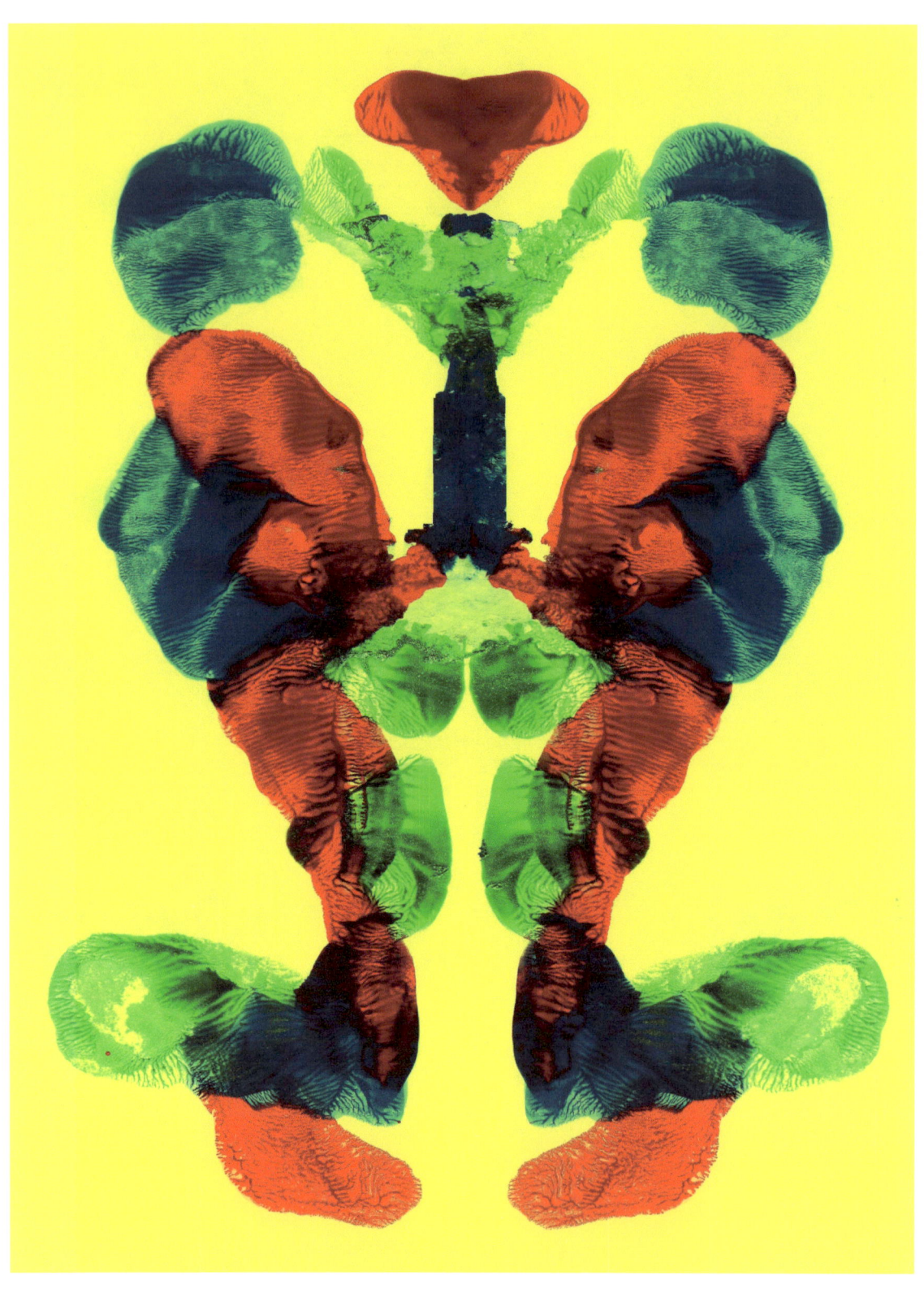

Image 10: Two people, a face, or ?

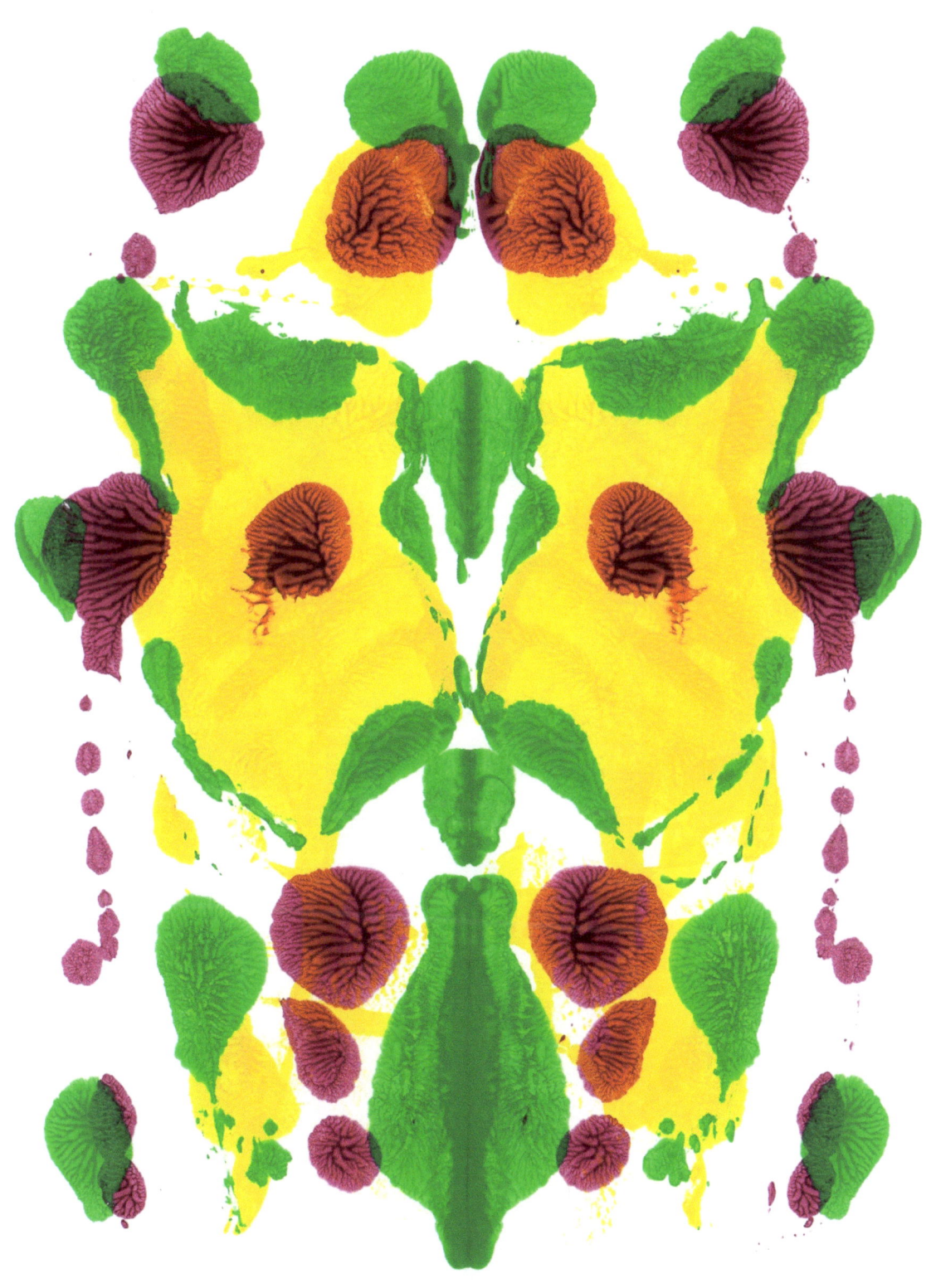

Image 11: Flowers, a person, or ?

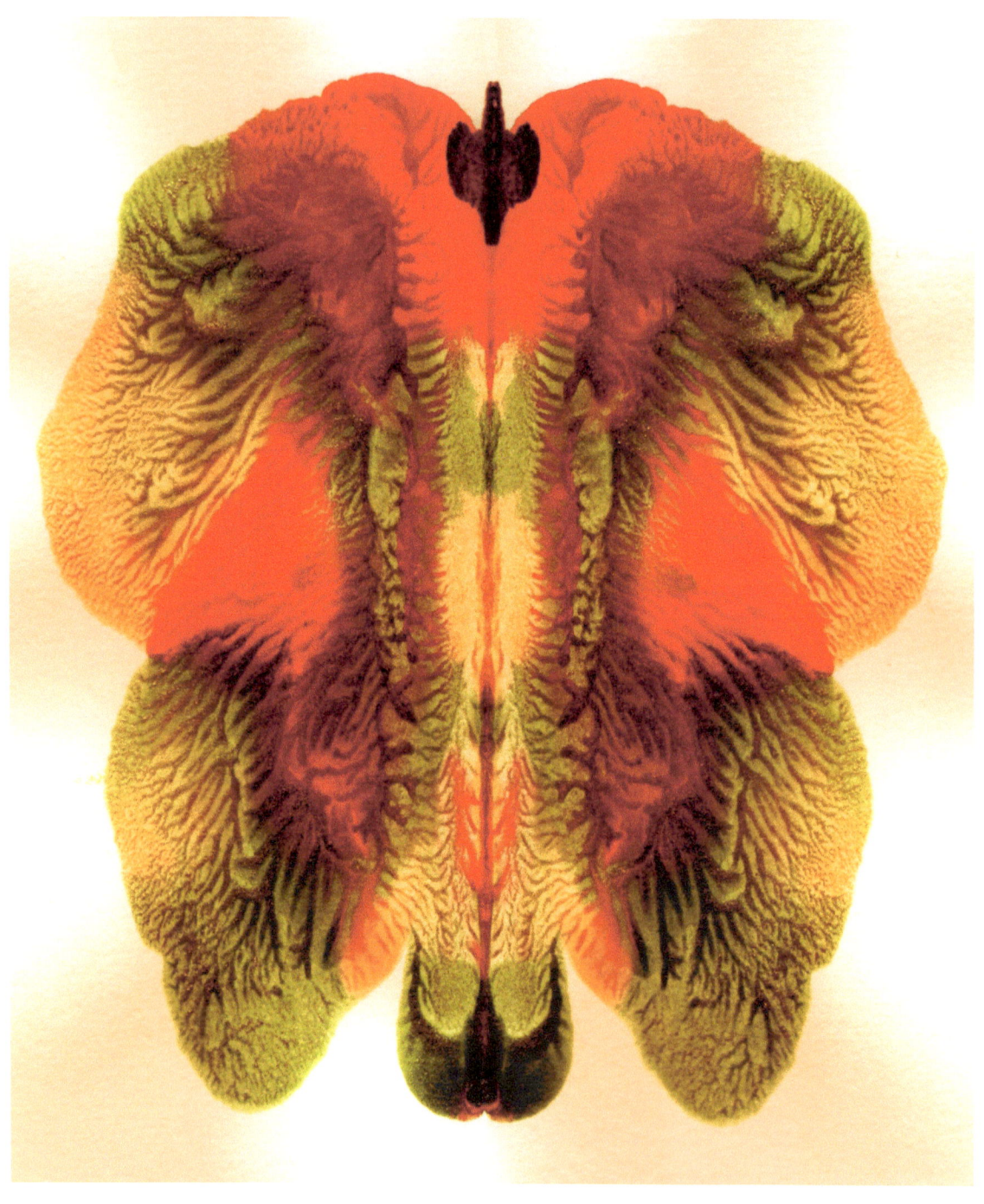

Image 12: A moth, goat face, or ?

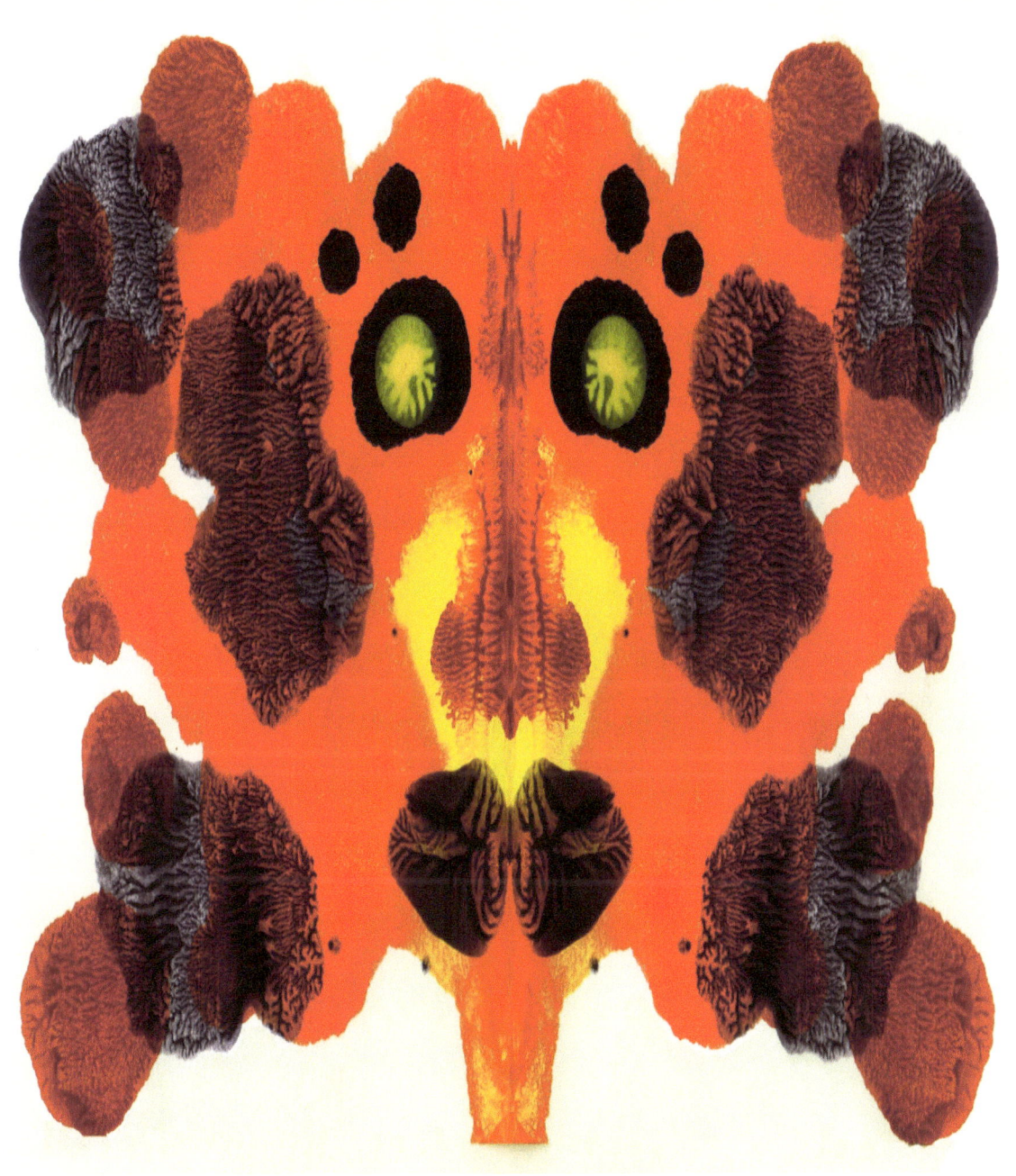

Image 13: A lion, masks, or ?

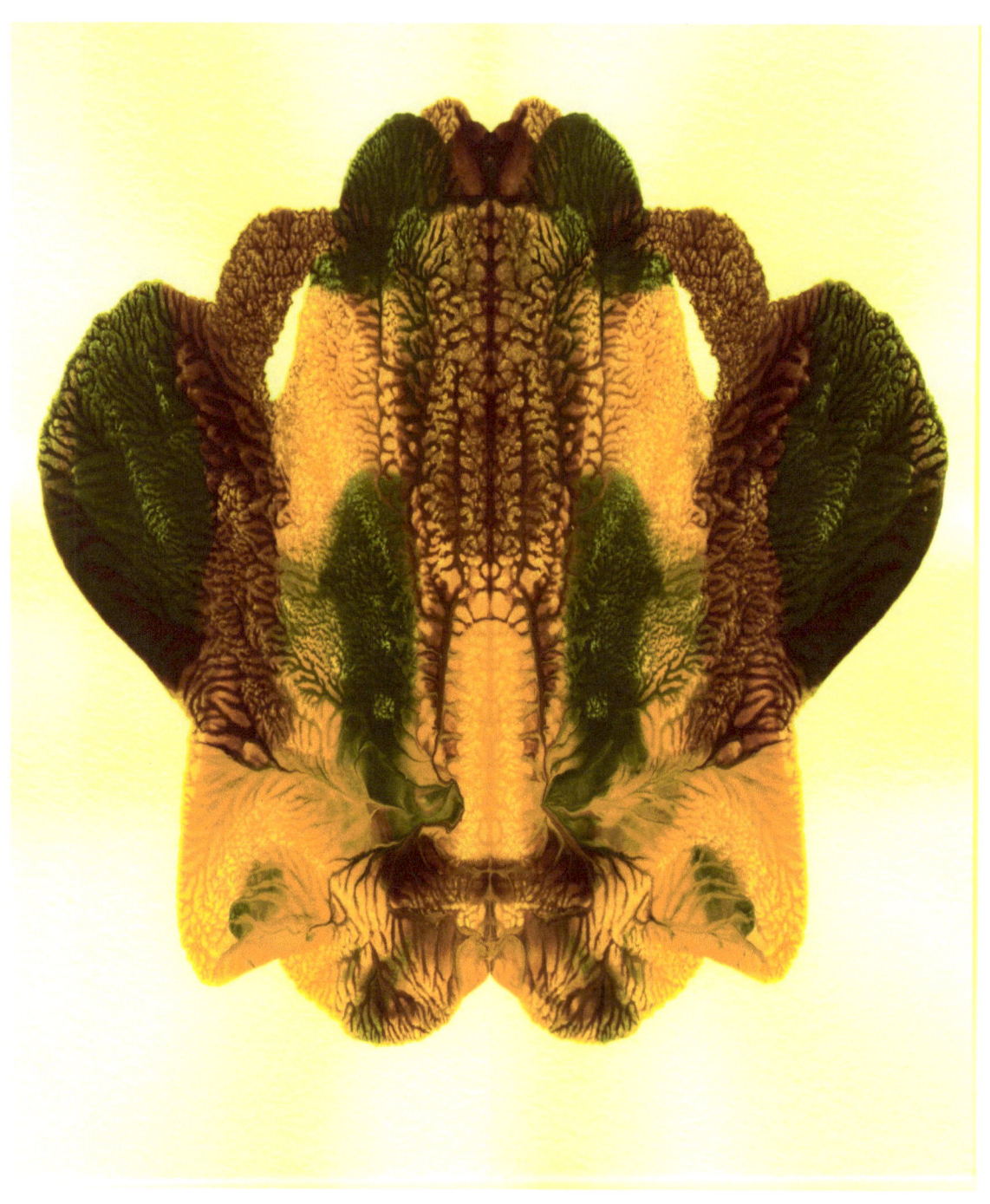

Image 14: A moth or ?

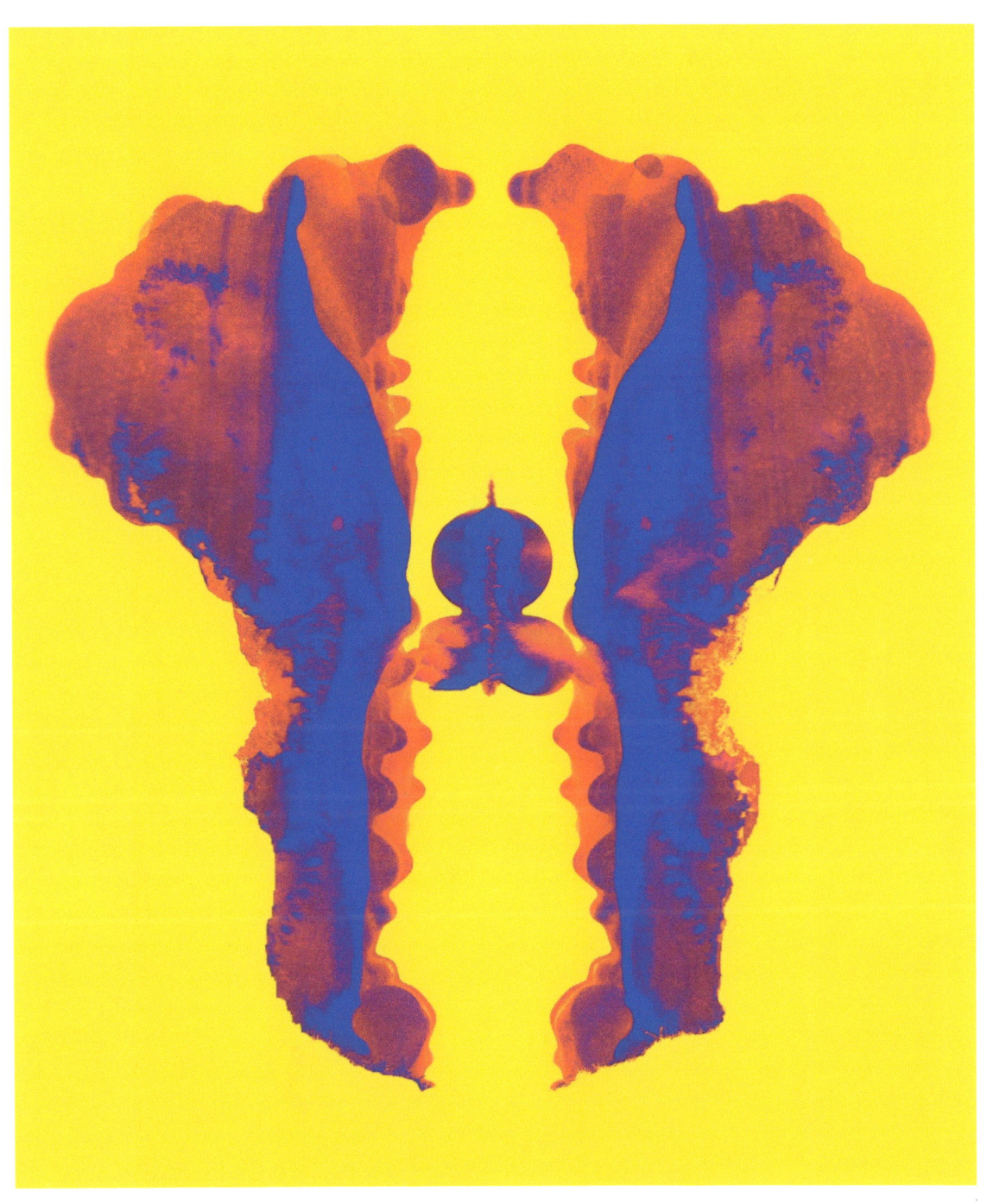

Image 15: An elephant, calf, or ?

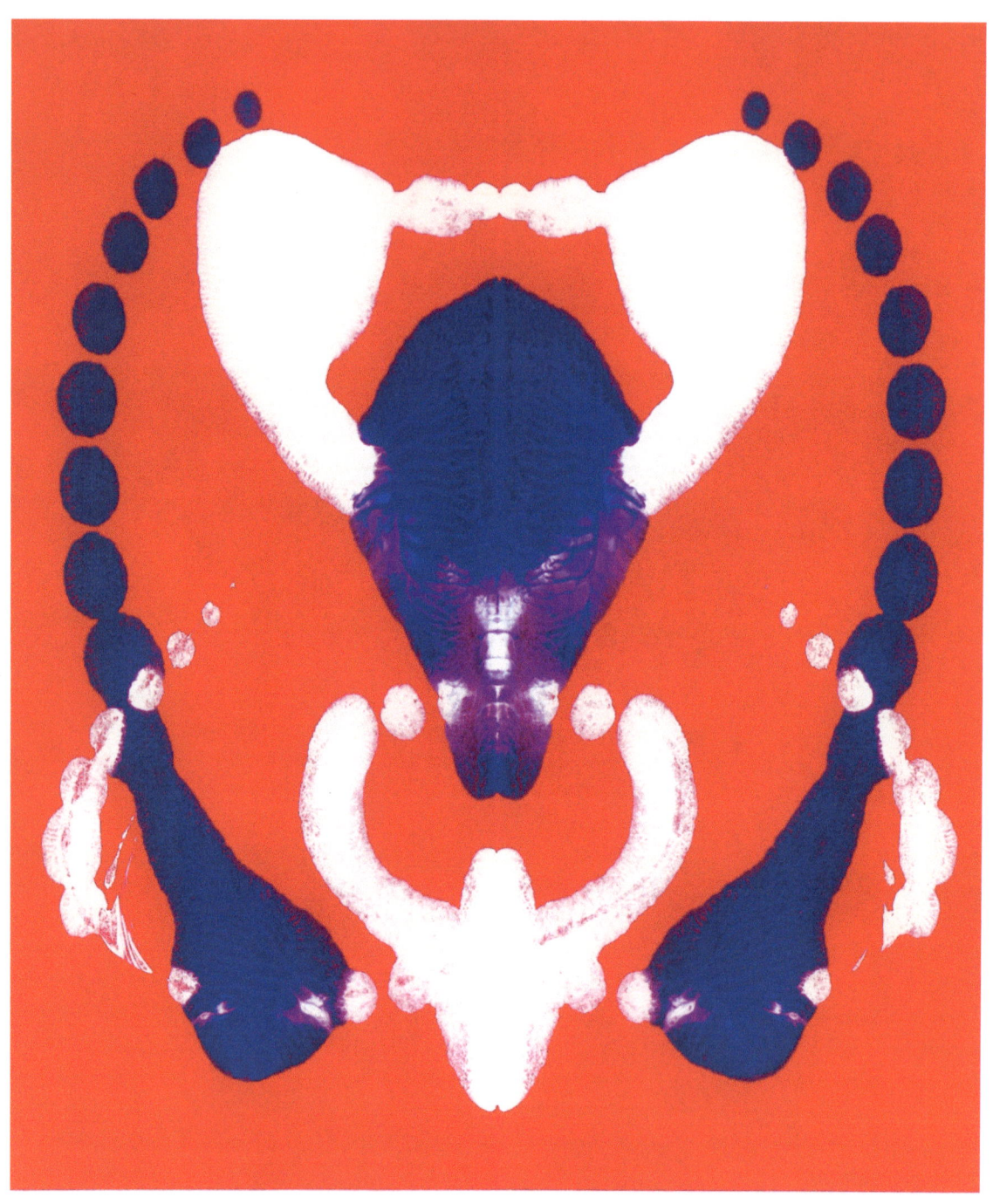

Image 16: Skulls, horns, or ?

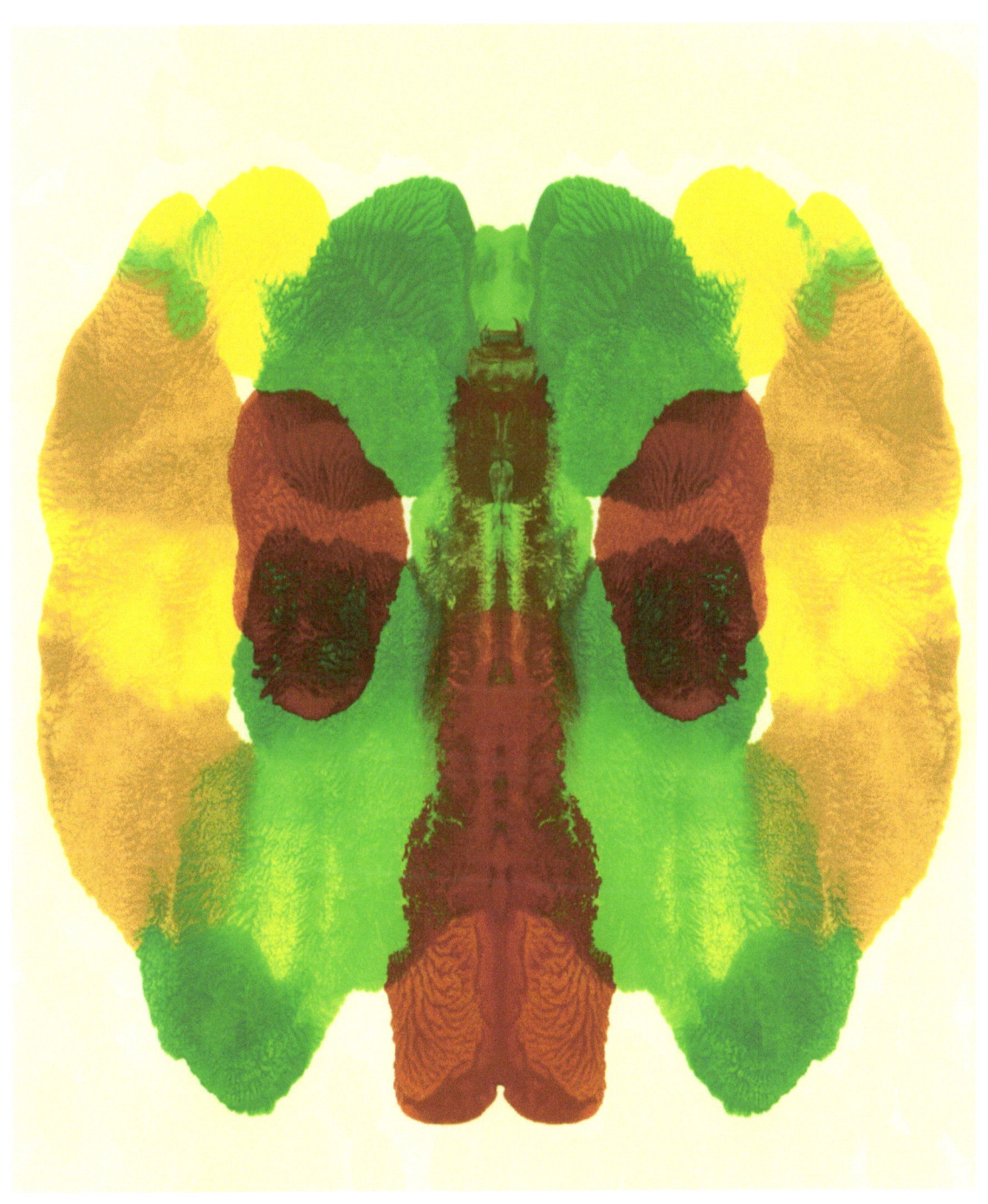

Image 17: A clown face, angel, or ?

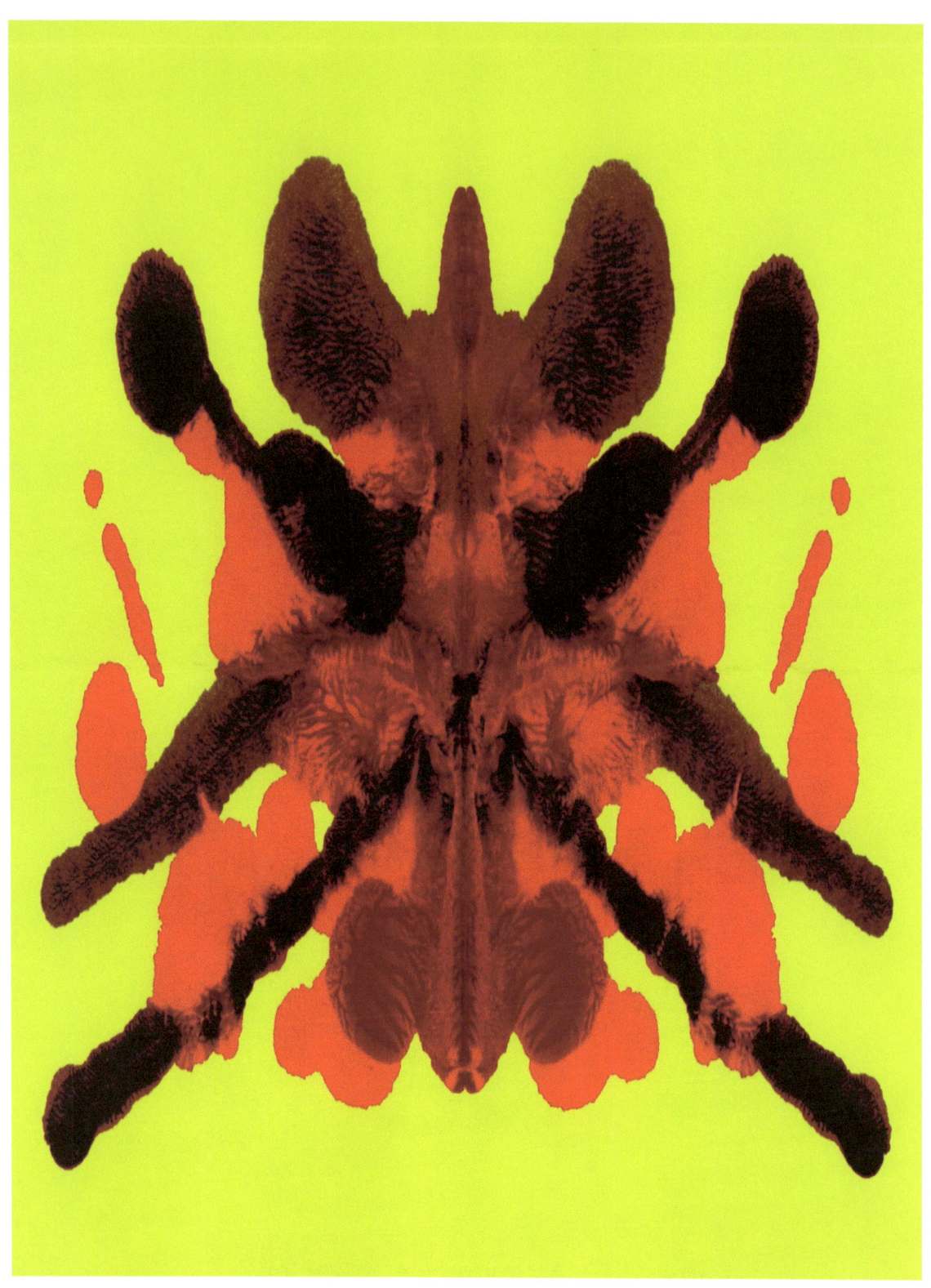

Image 18: A bat, flames, or ?

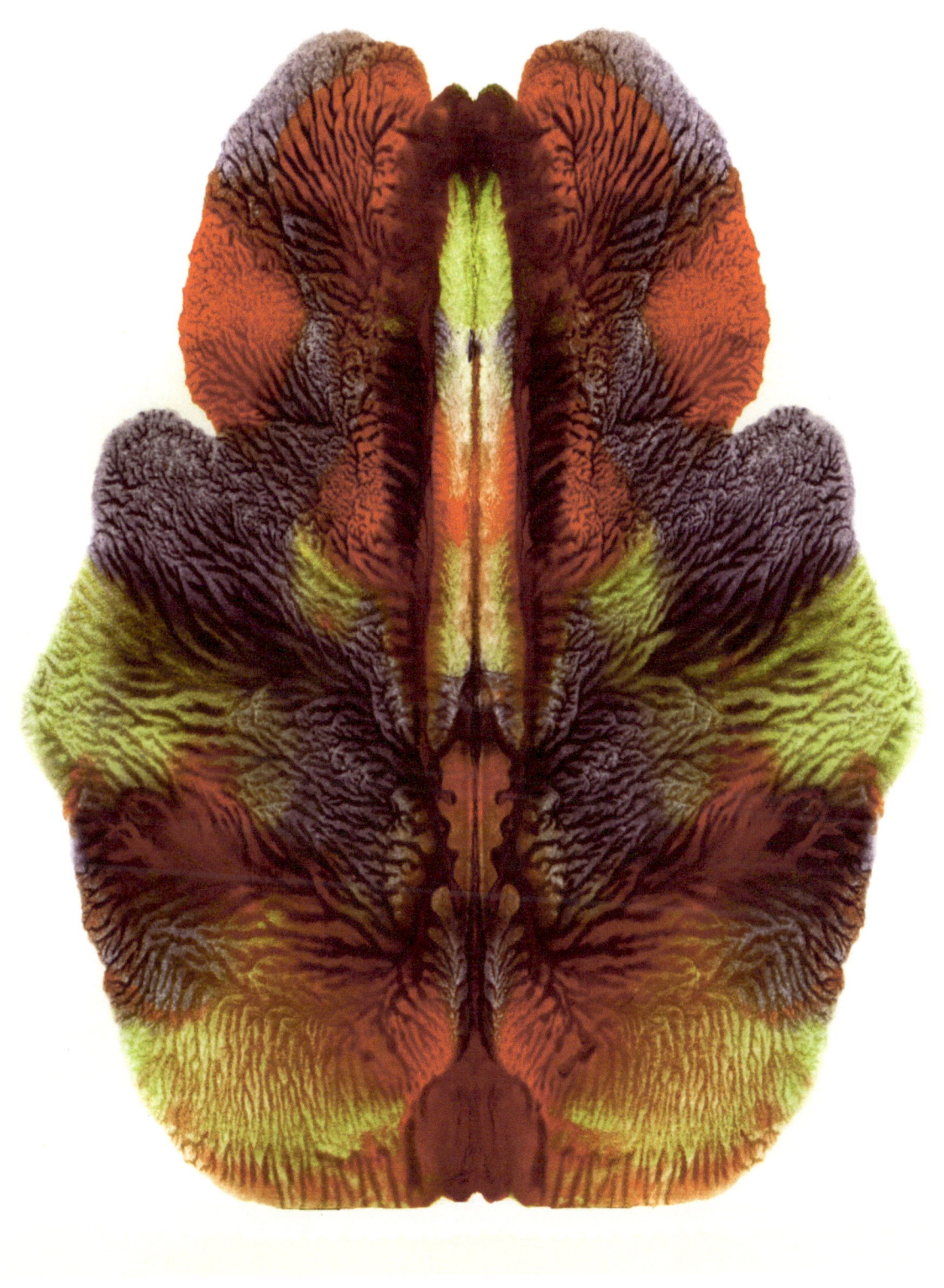

Image 19: A possum, exposed bottom, or ?

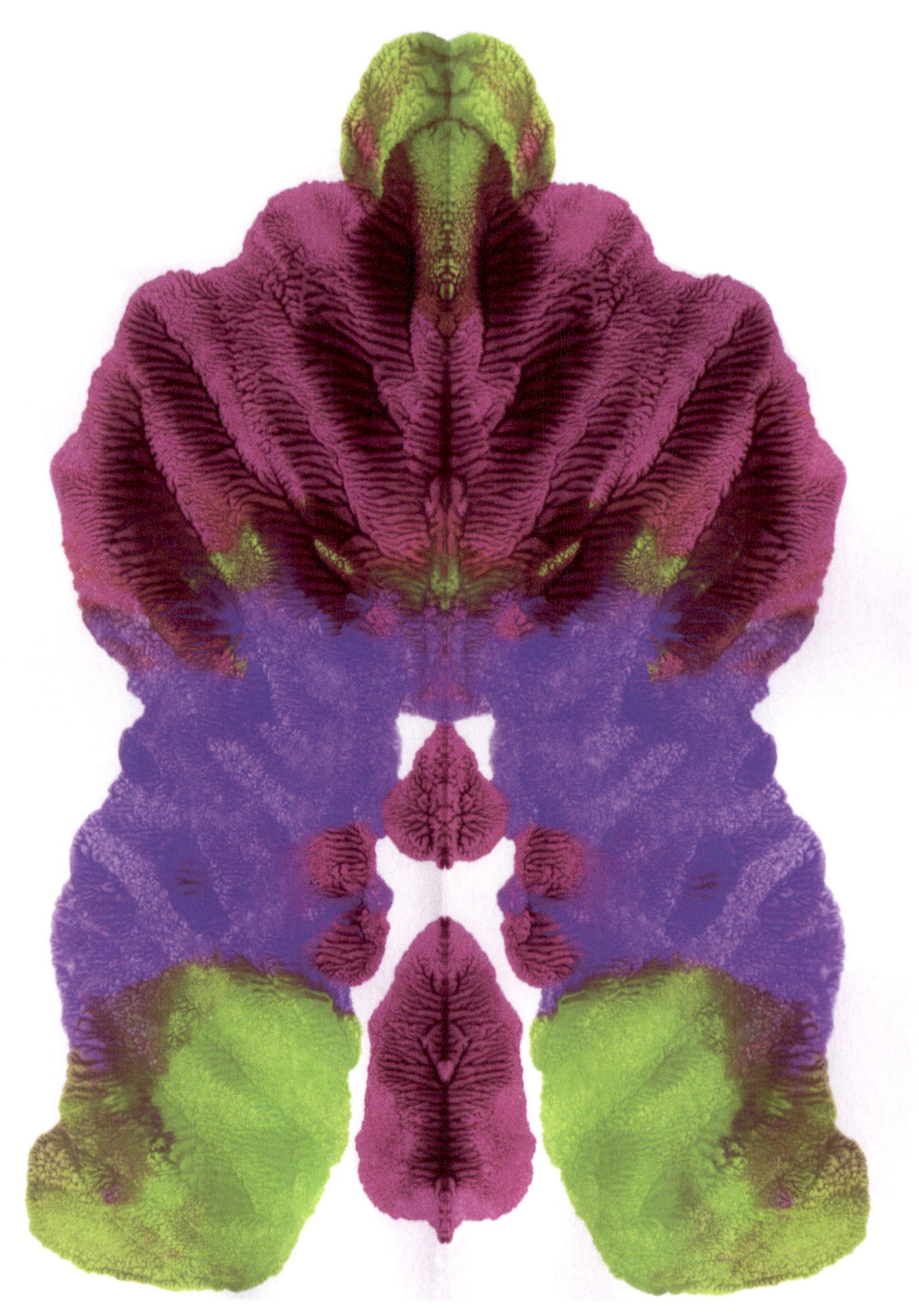

Image 20: A sensei, alien, or ?

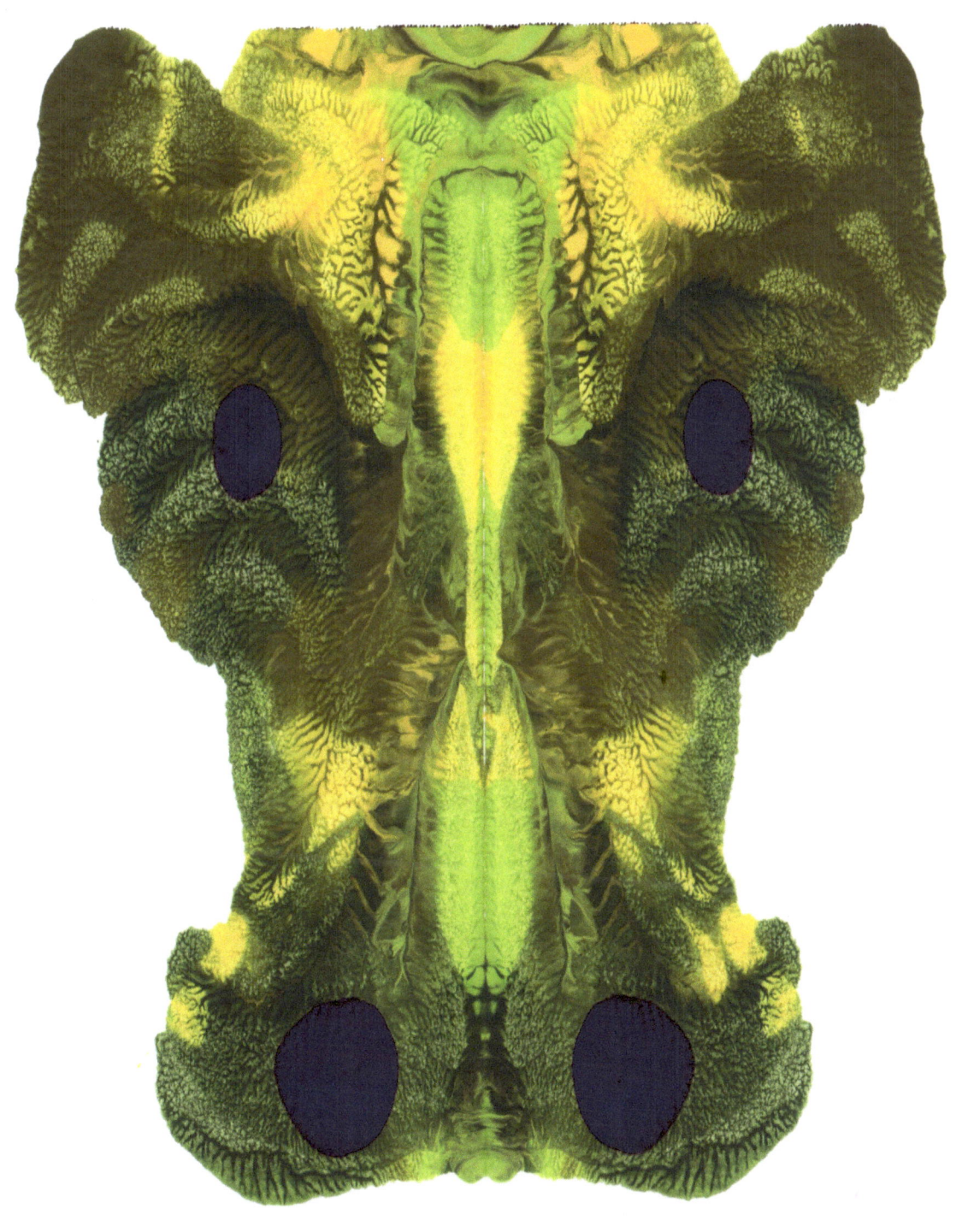

Image 21: An alligator, cow, or ?

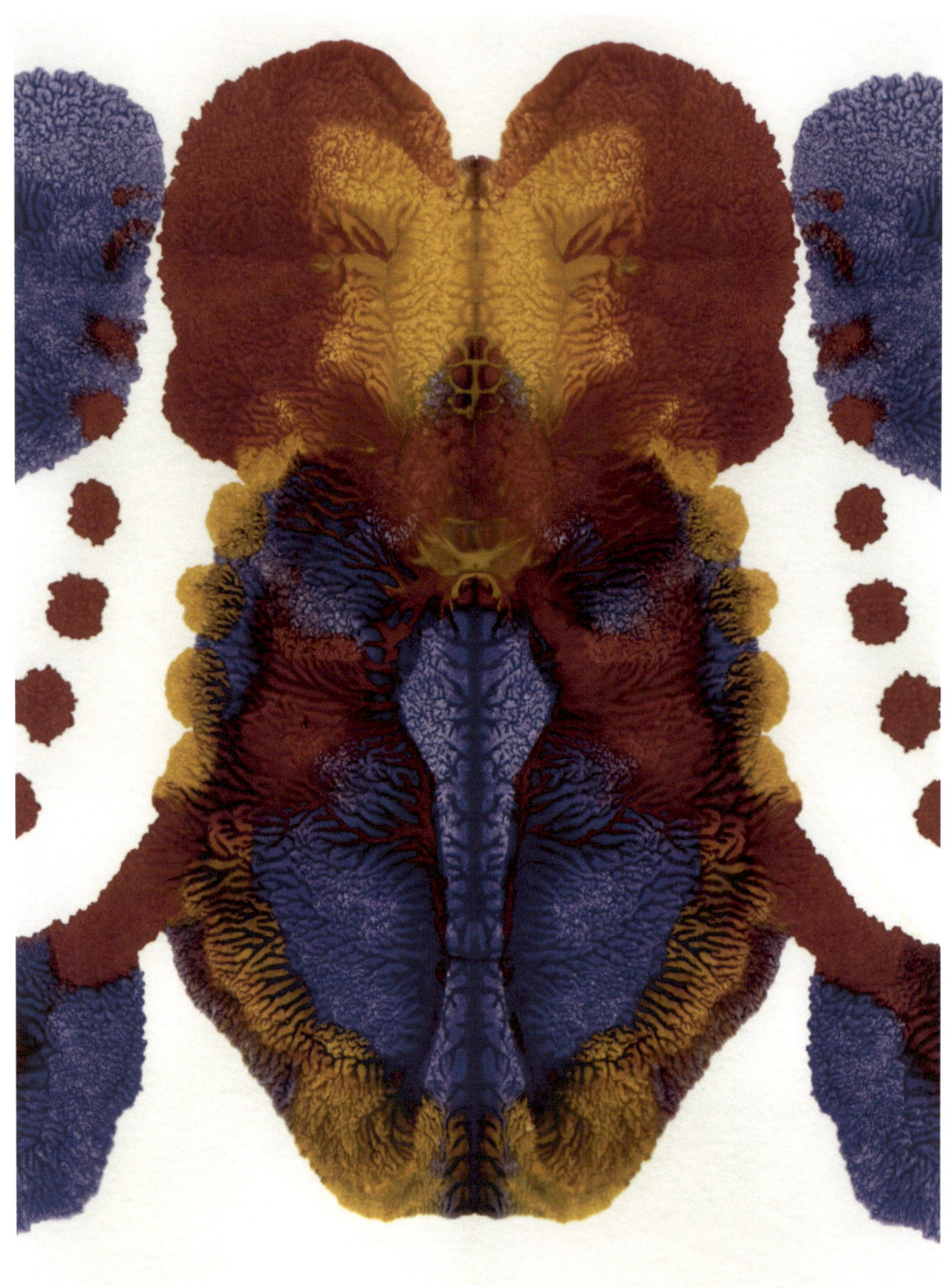

Image 22: A poodle or ?

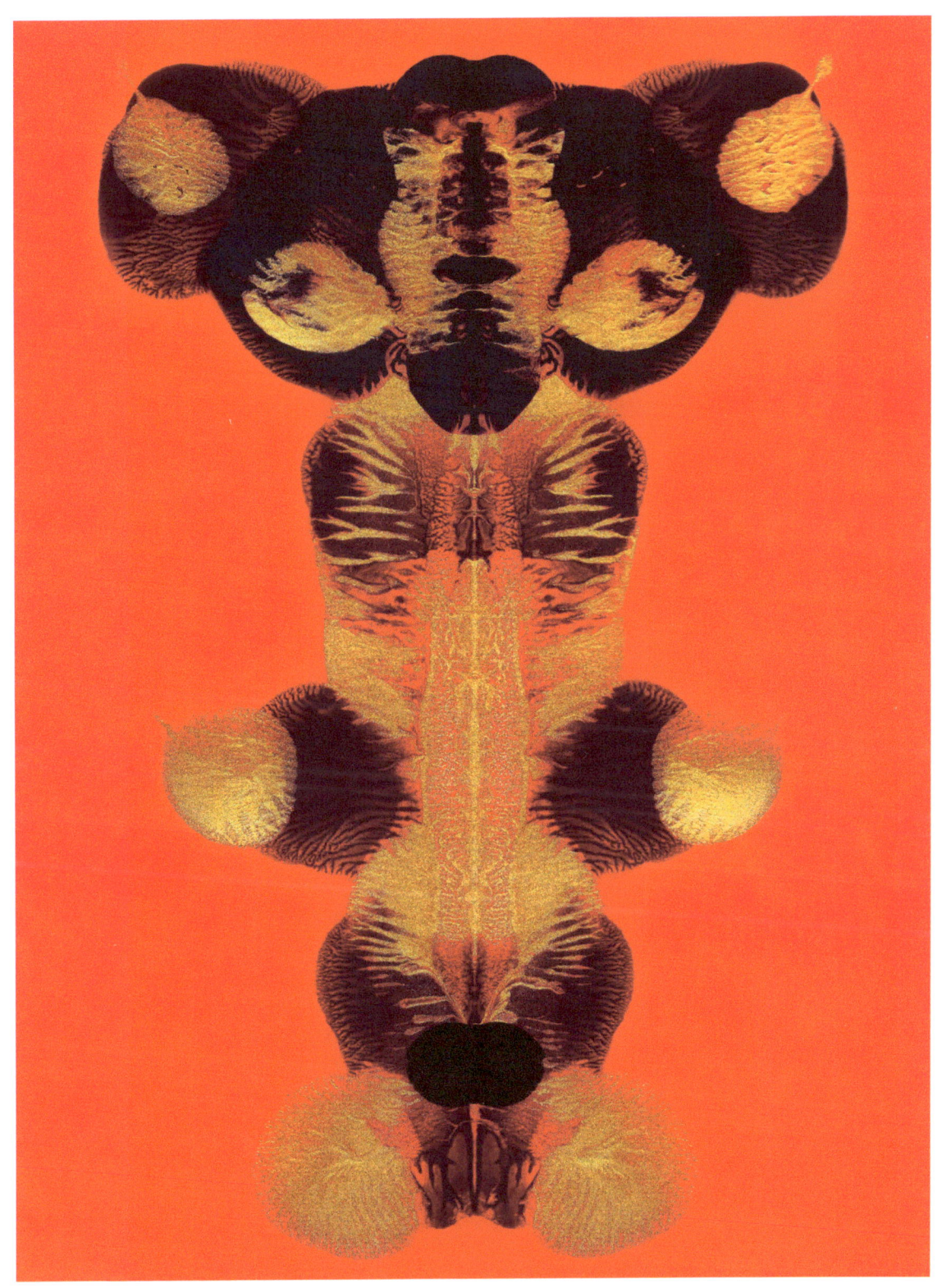

Image 23: A Siamese cat or ?

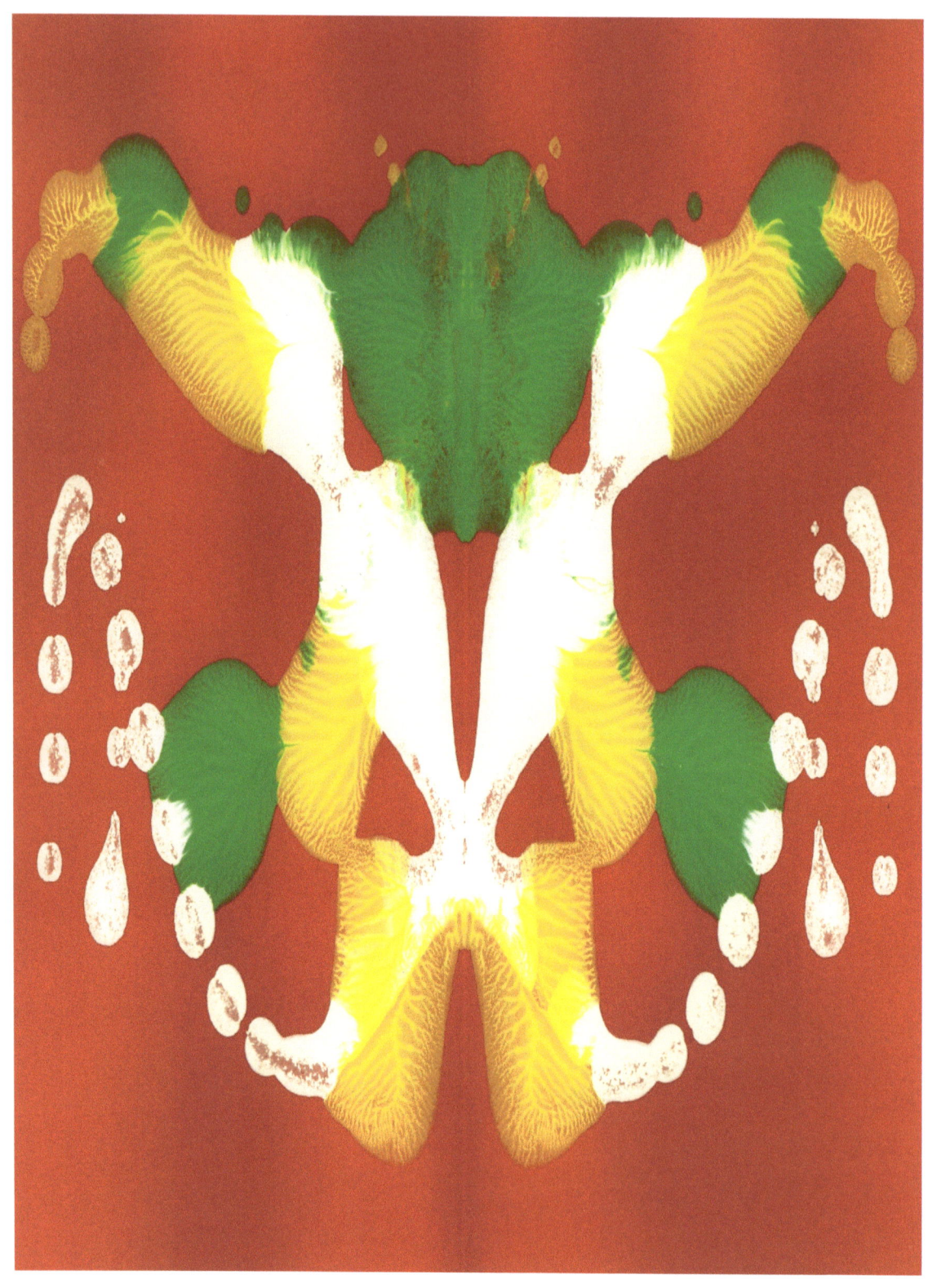

Image 24: A mask, kung fu master, or ?

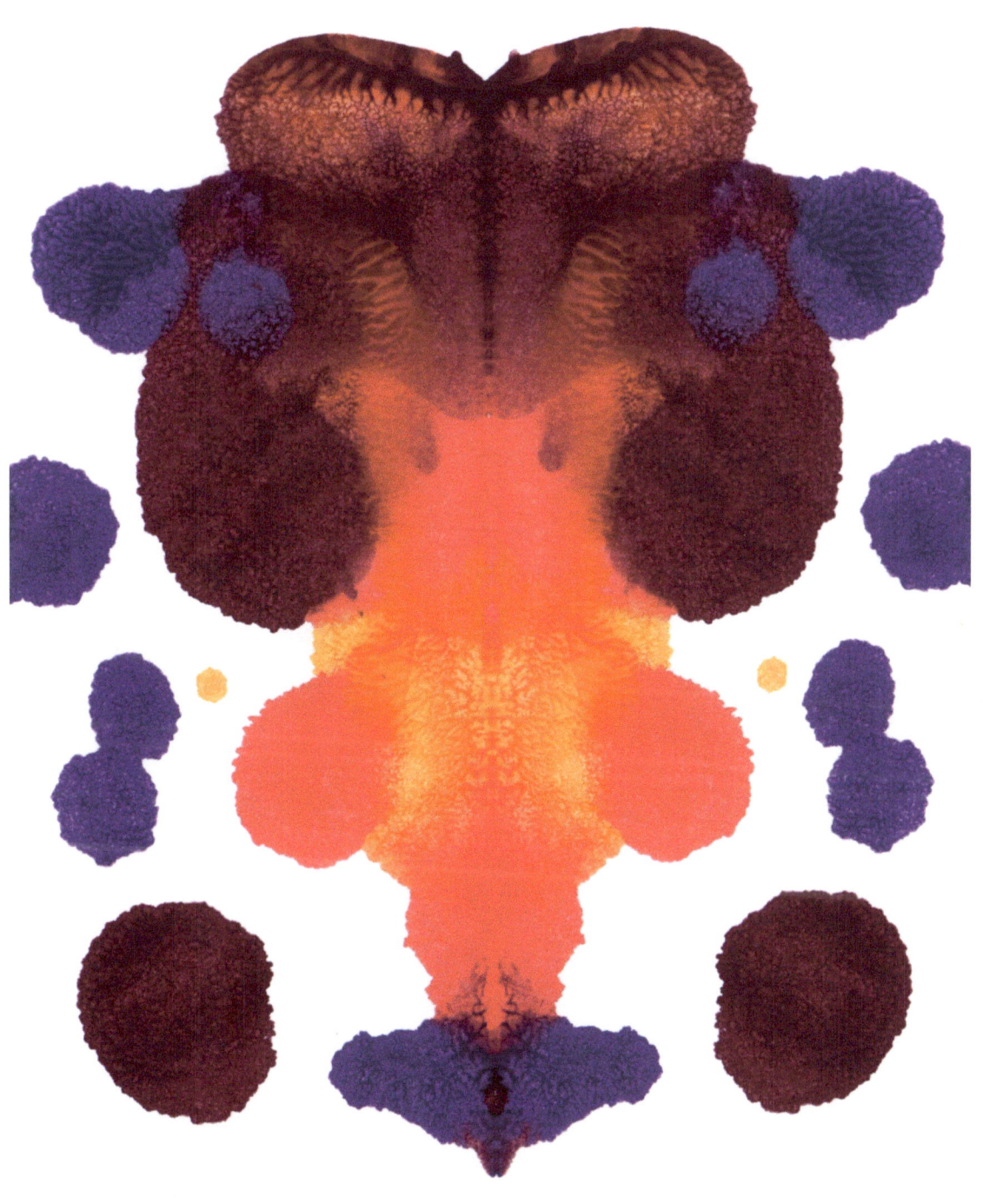

Image 25: A warthog or ?

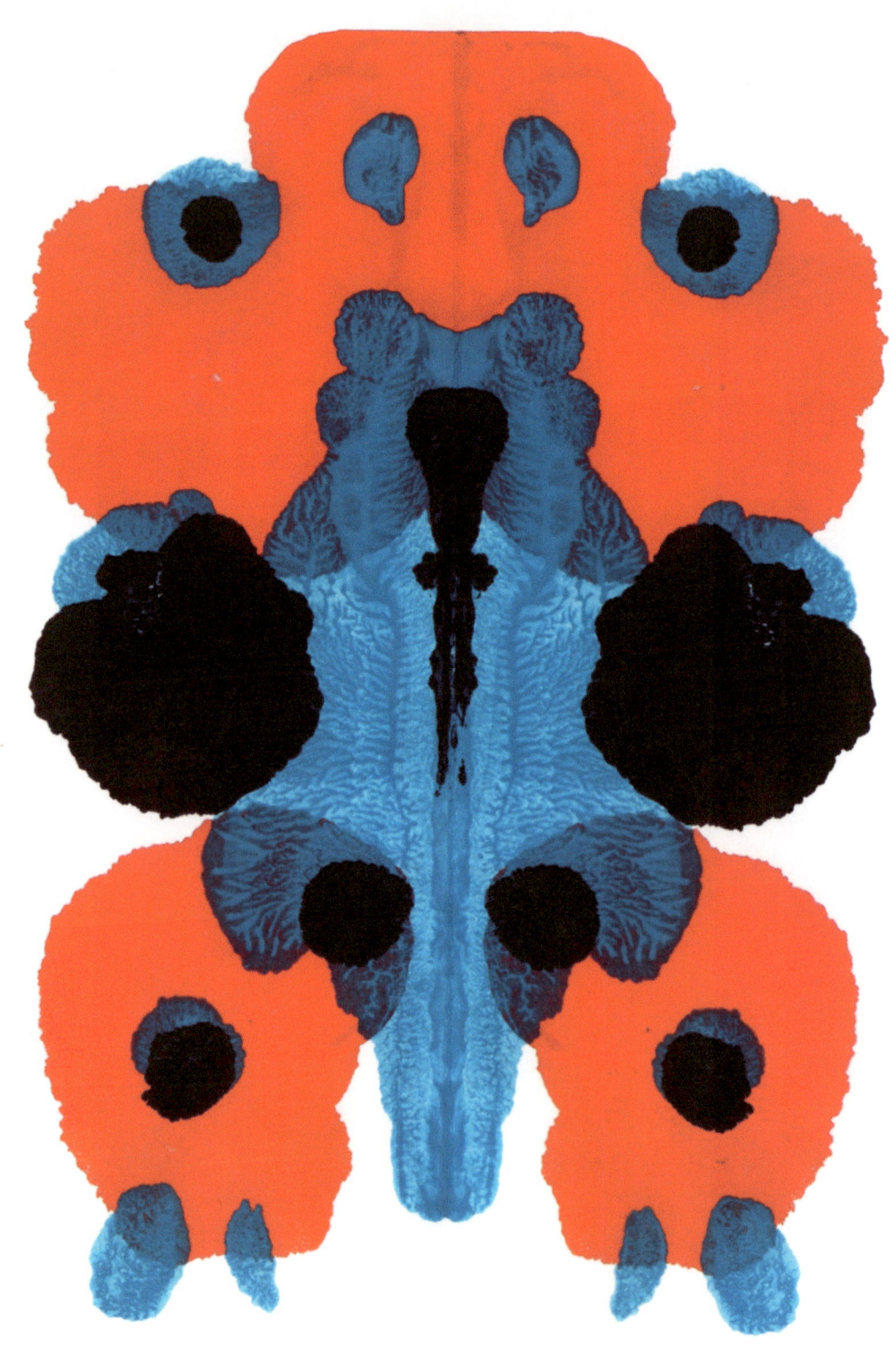

Image 26: A walrus, beaver, or ?

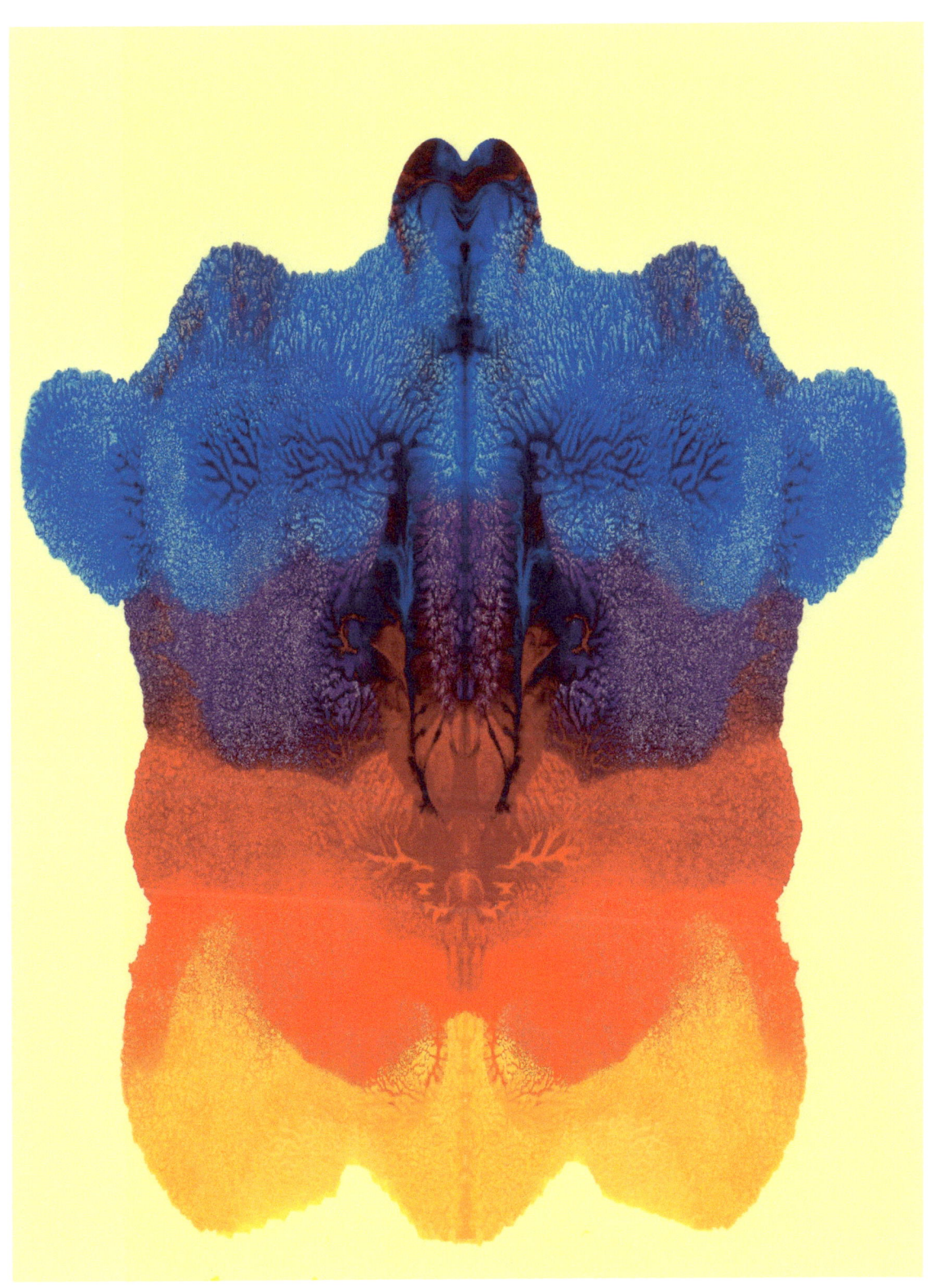

Image 27: A face, gorilla, or ?

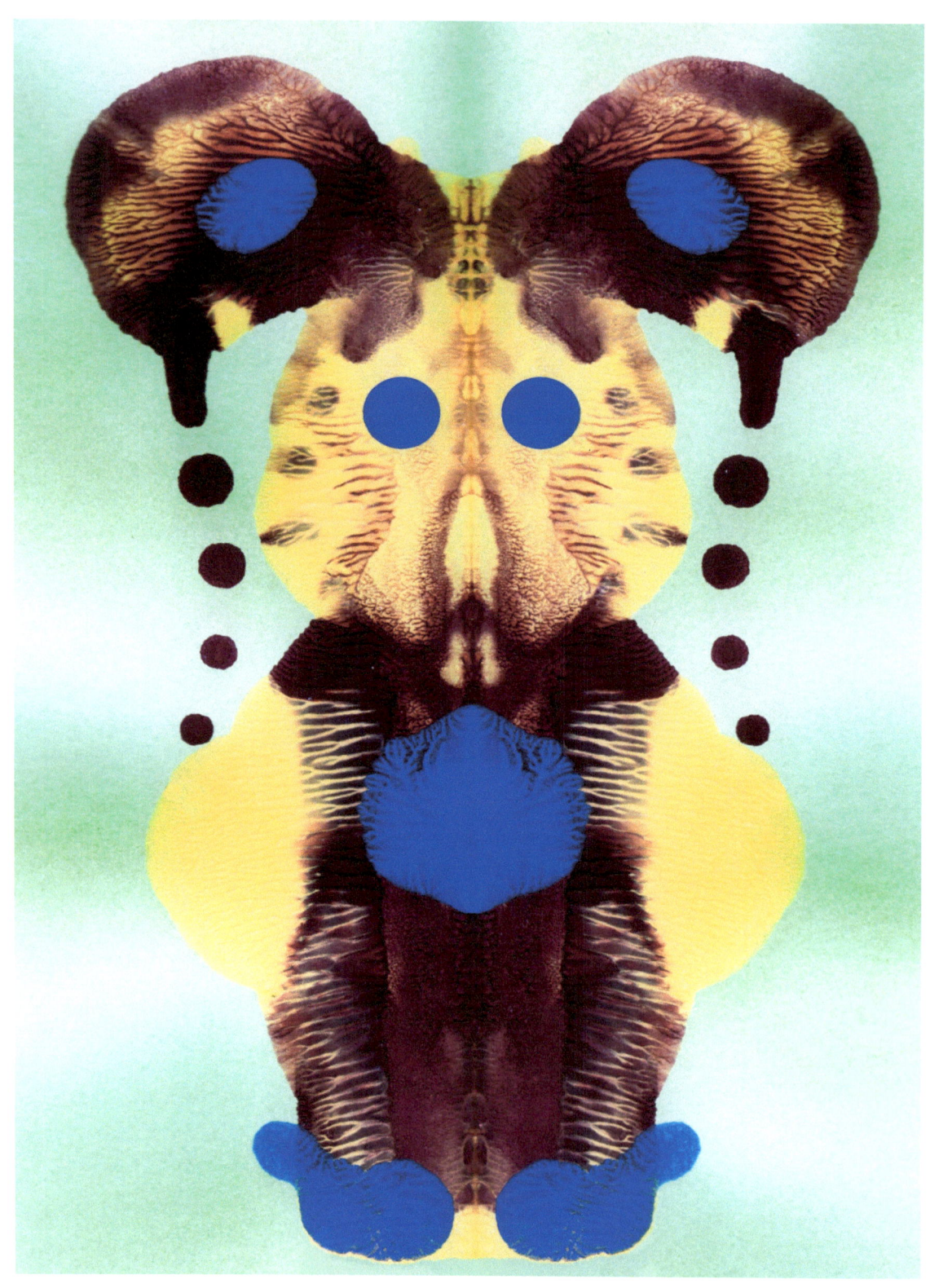

Image 28: A rabbit in a dress or ?

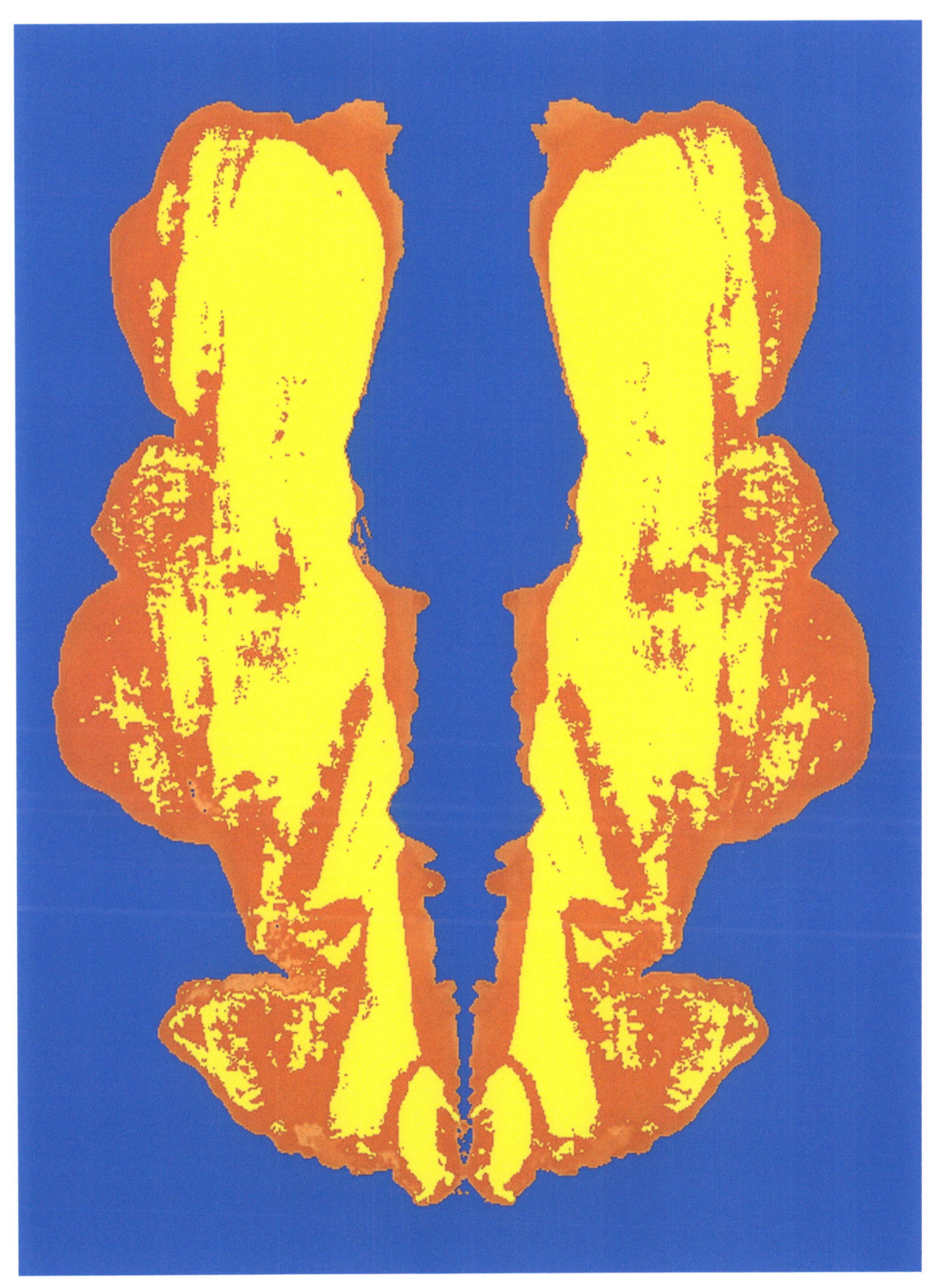

Image 29: A face, lobster, or ?

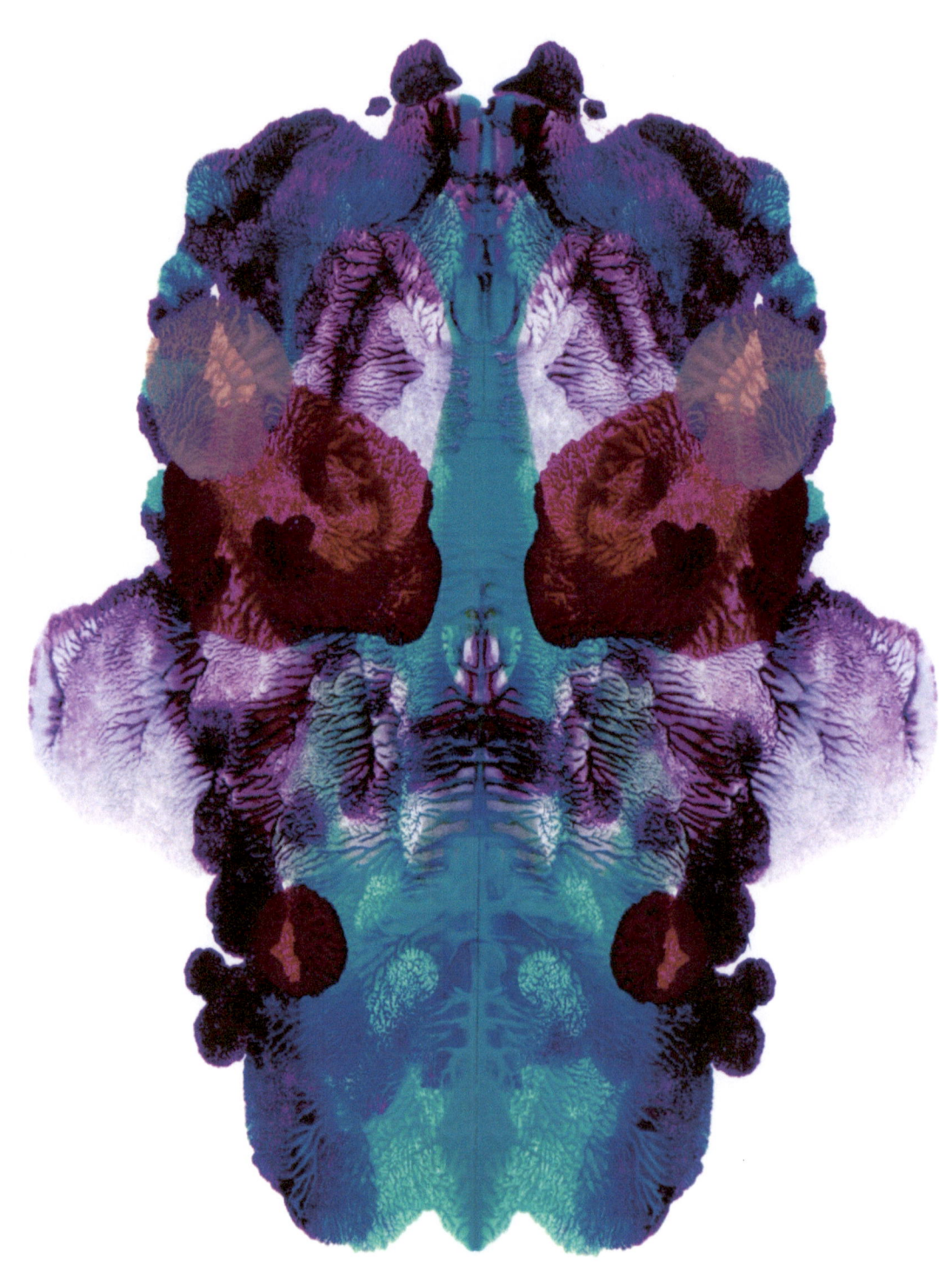

Image 30: Frankenstein or ?

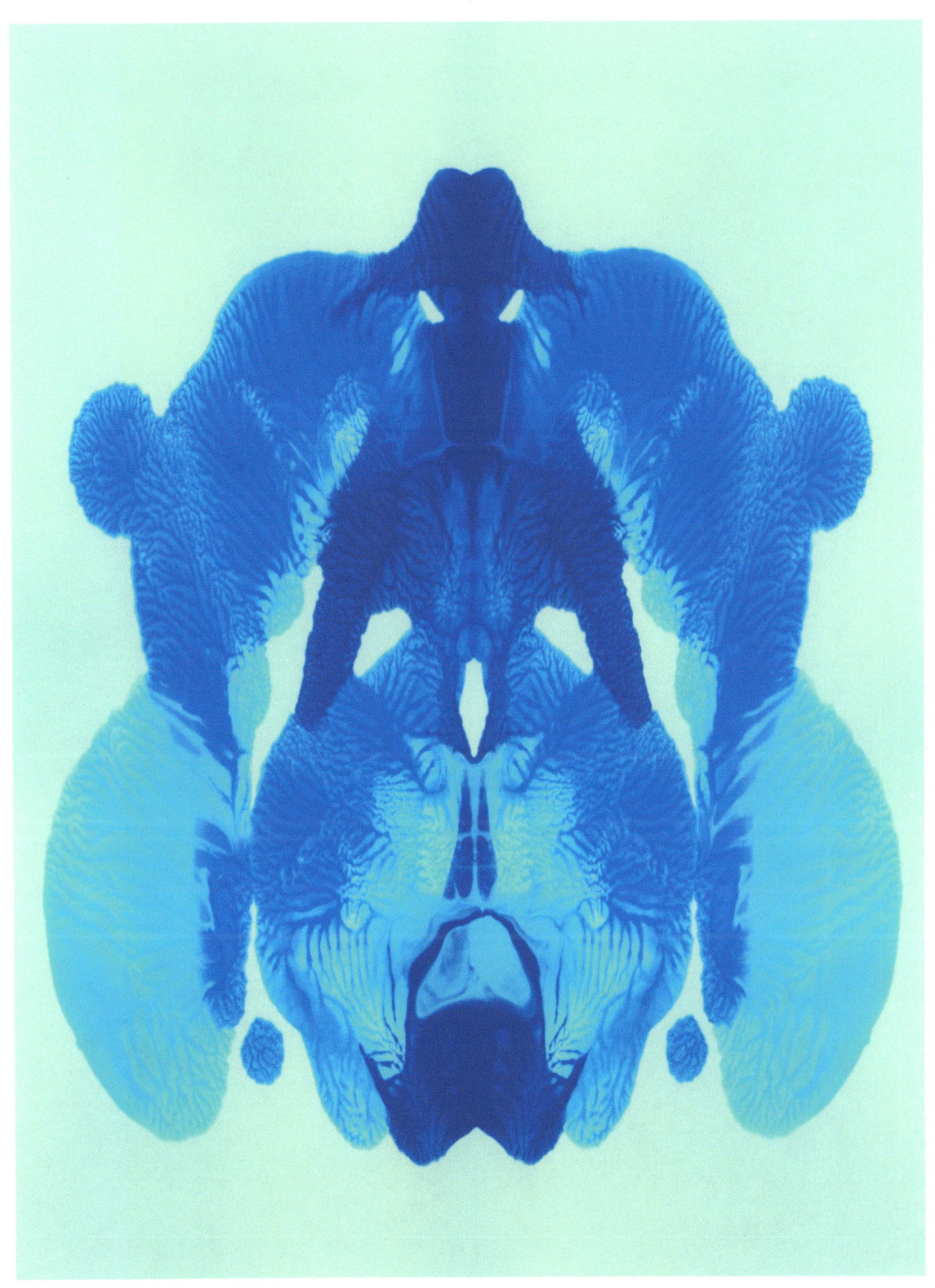

Image 31: A matador, bear, or ?

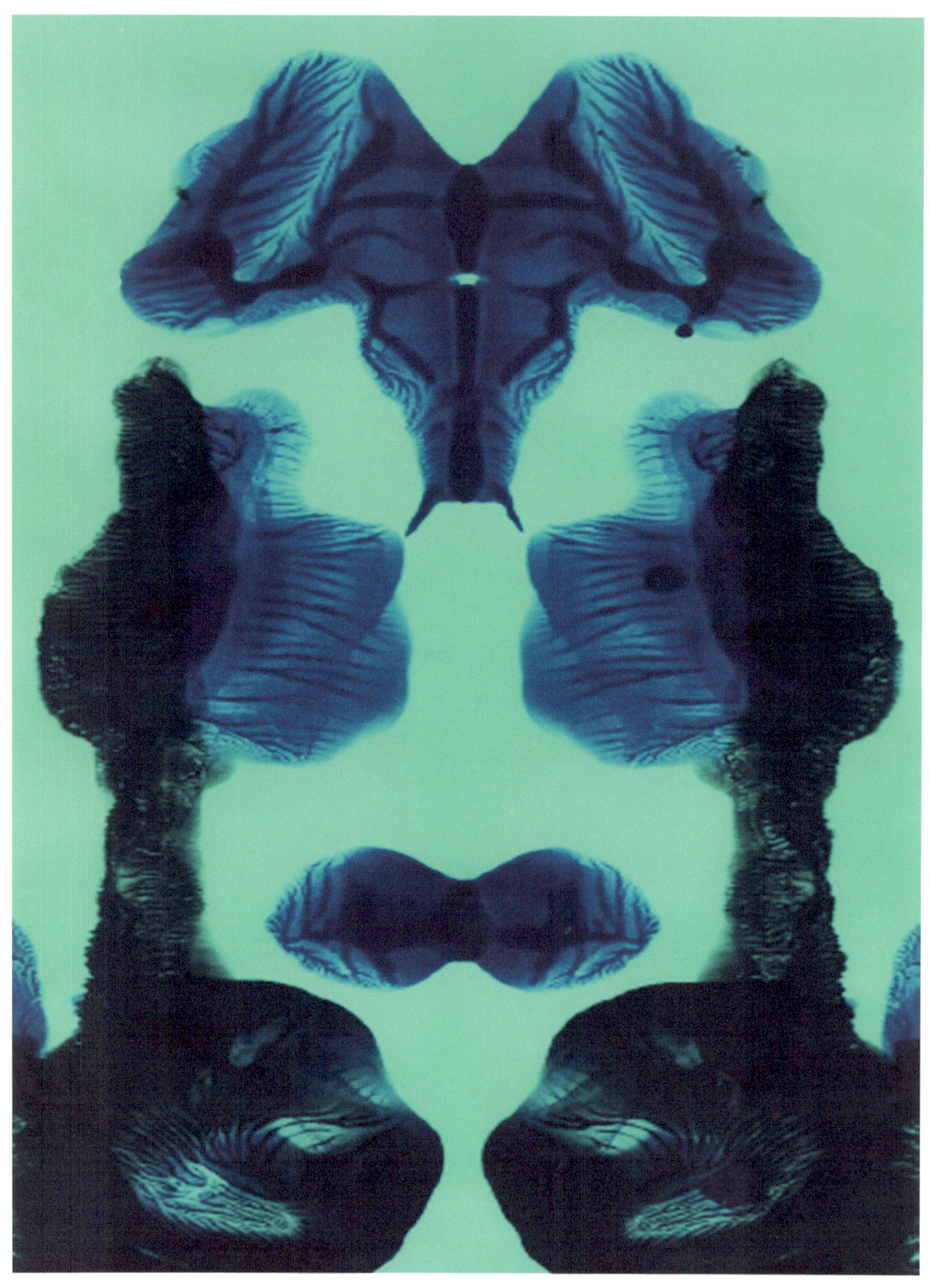

Image 32: A person, dogs, or ?

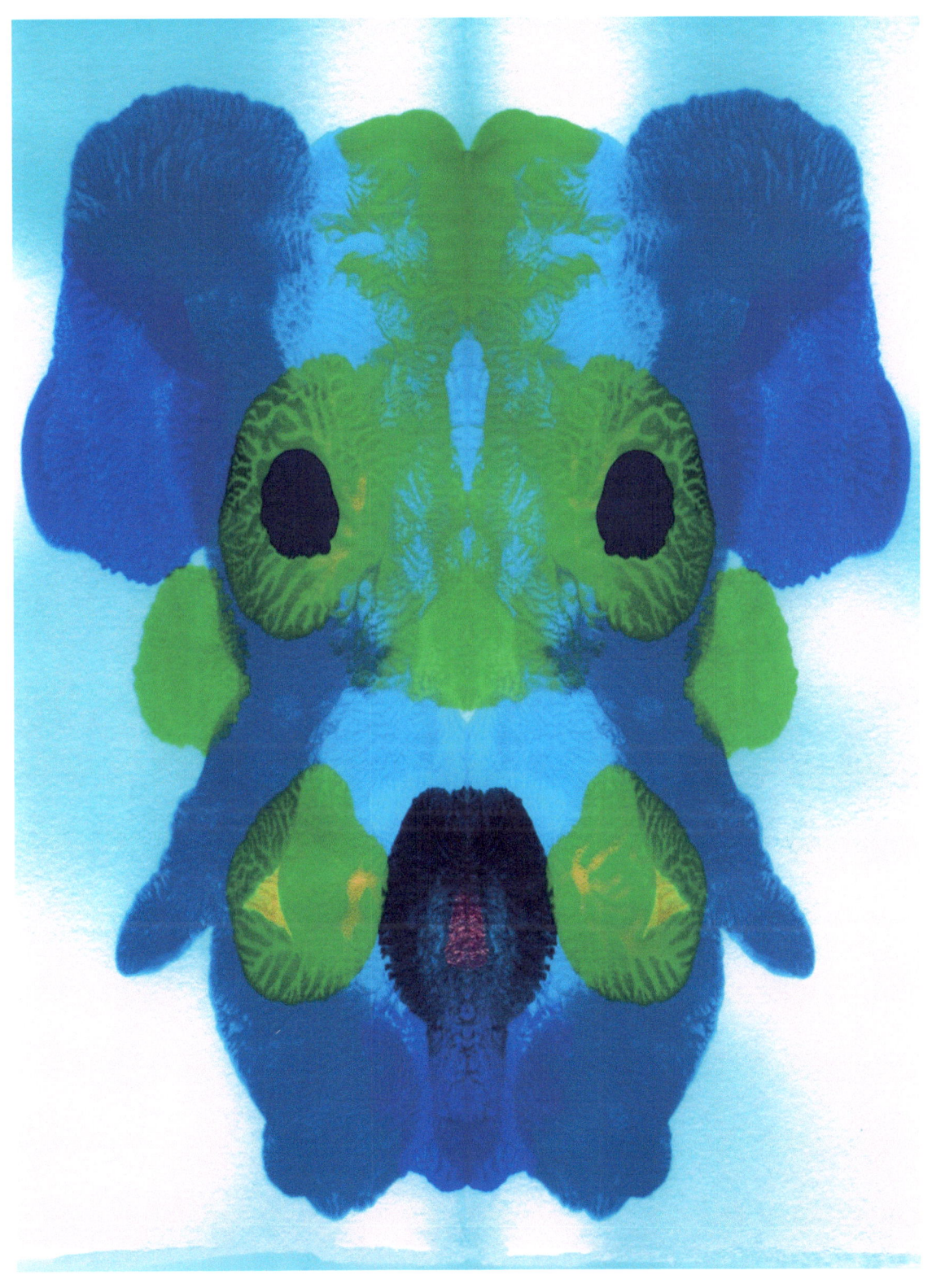

Image 33: Two lambs, a puppy, or ?

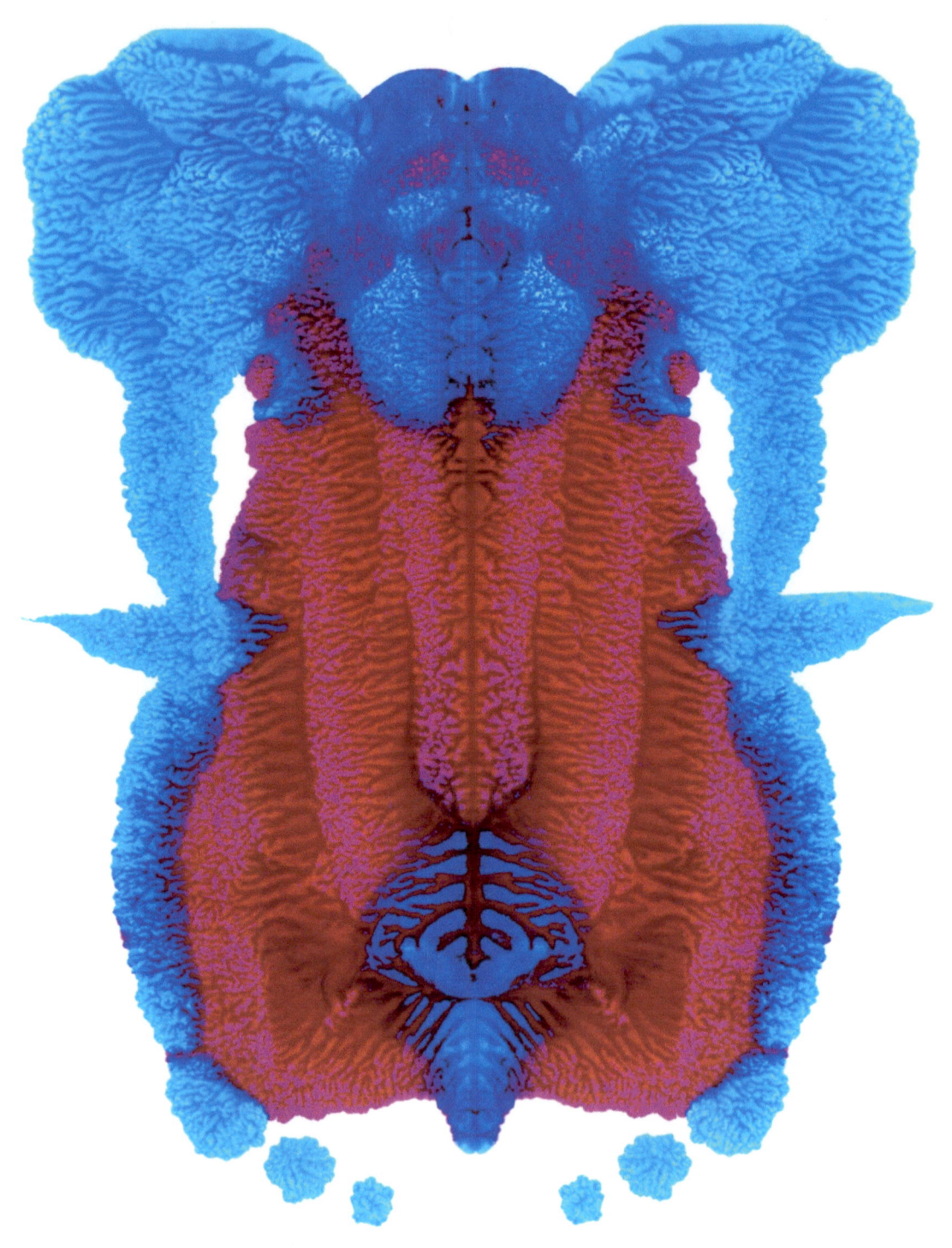

Image 34: A goat, face, or ?

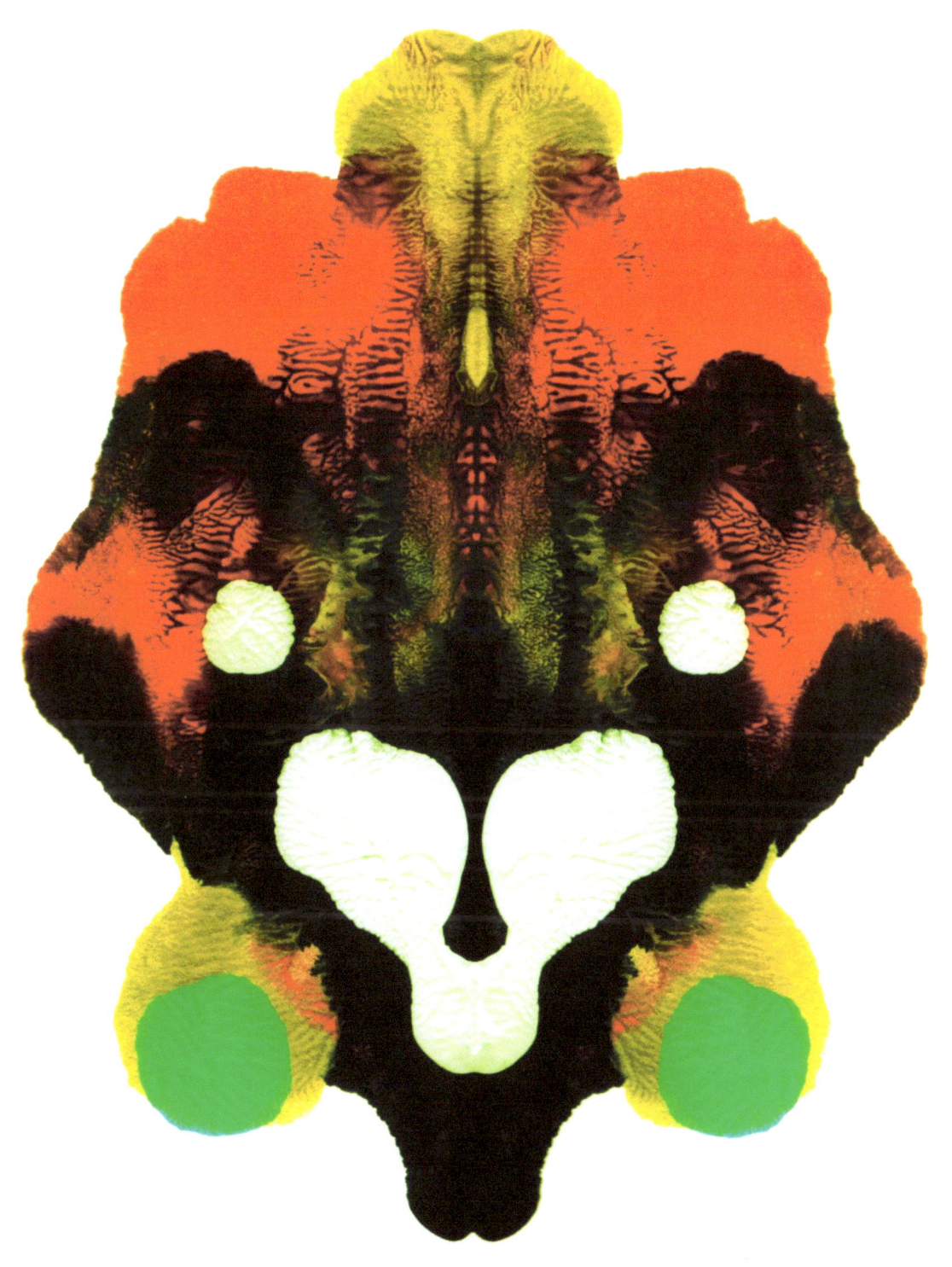

Image 35: A bird or ?

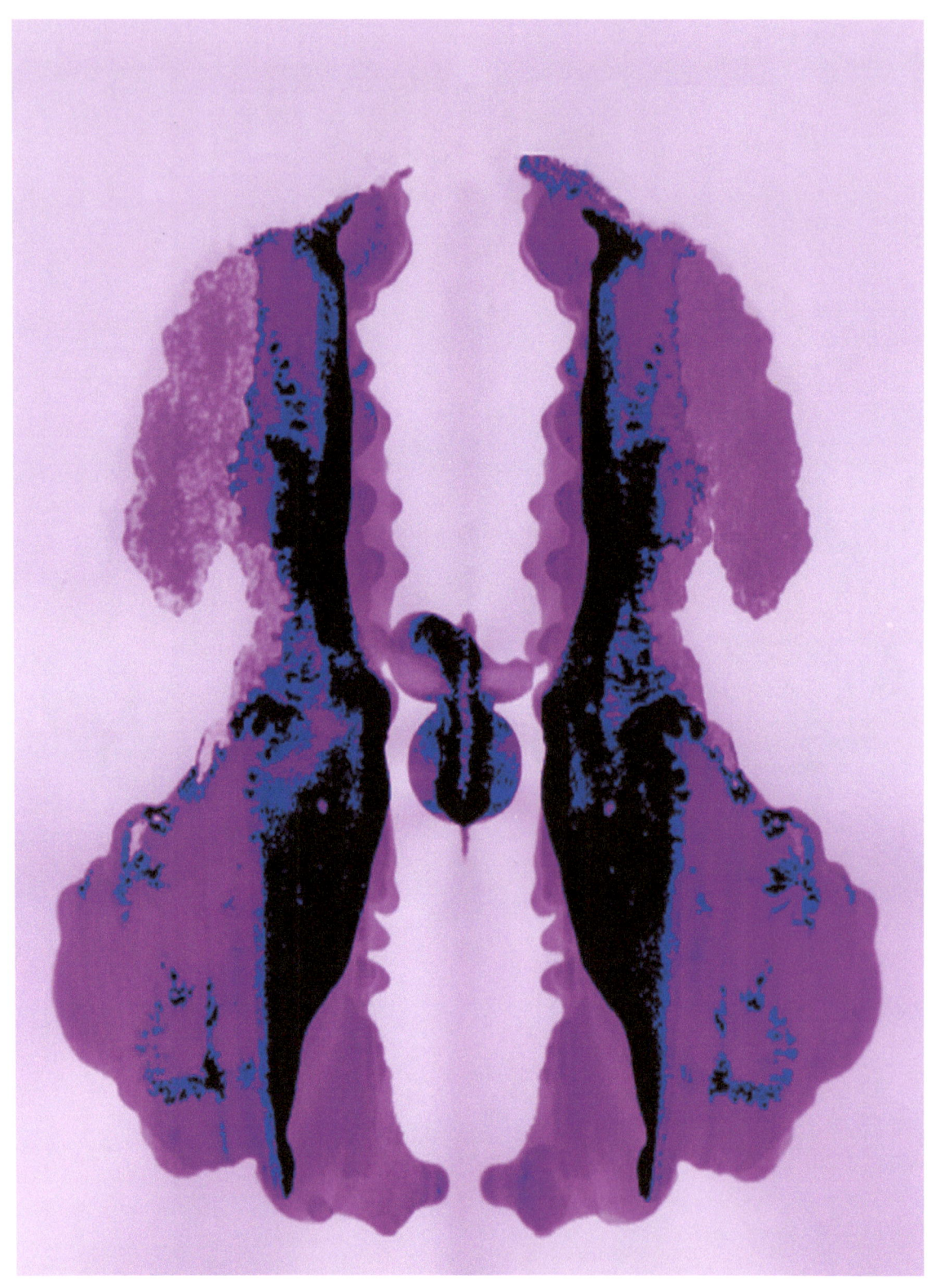

Image 36: A party dress, dog, or ?

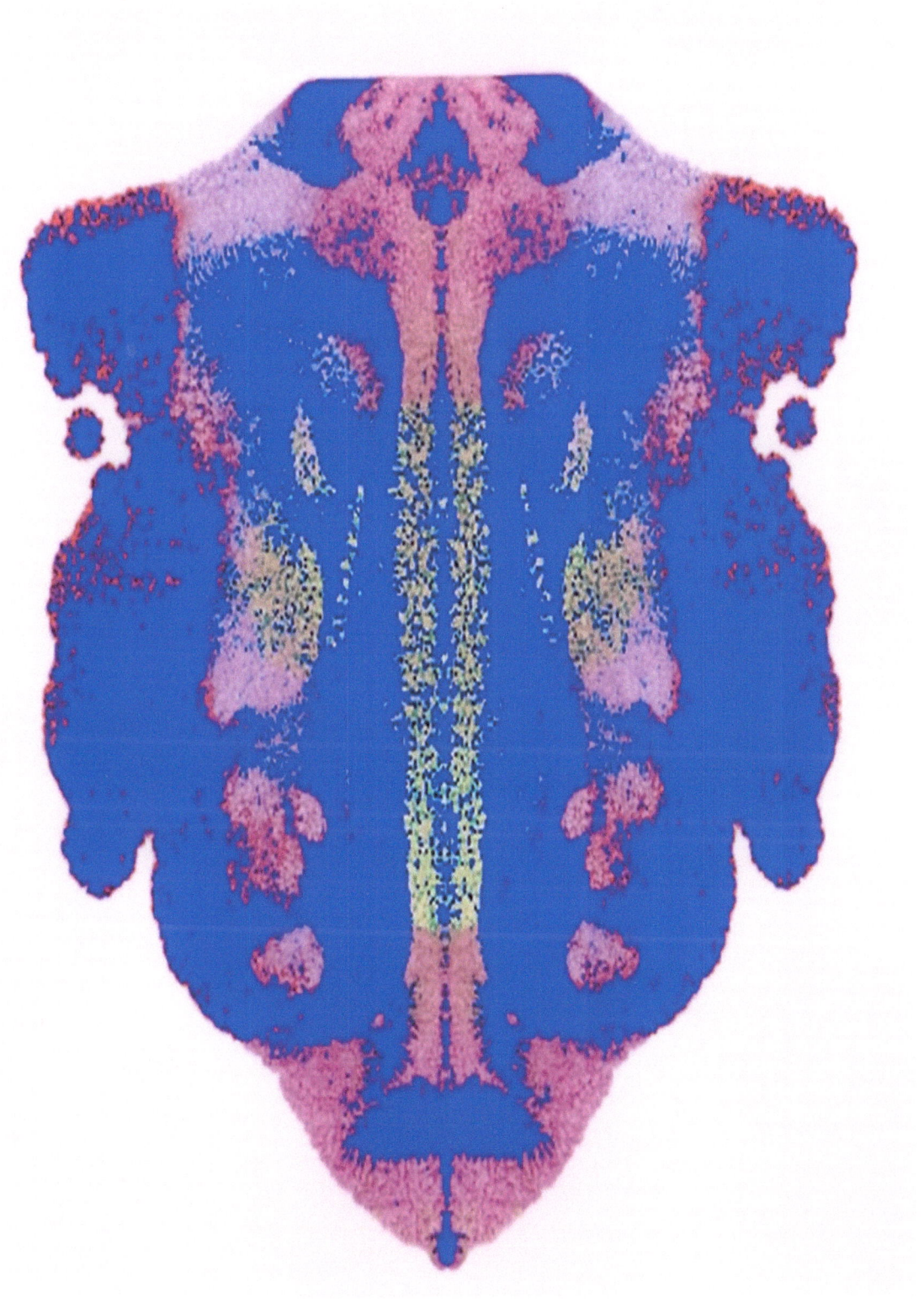

Image 37: An elongated body, face, or ?

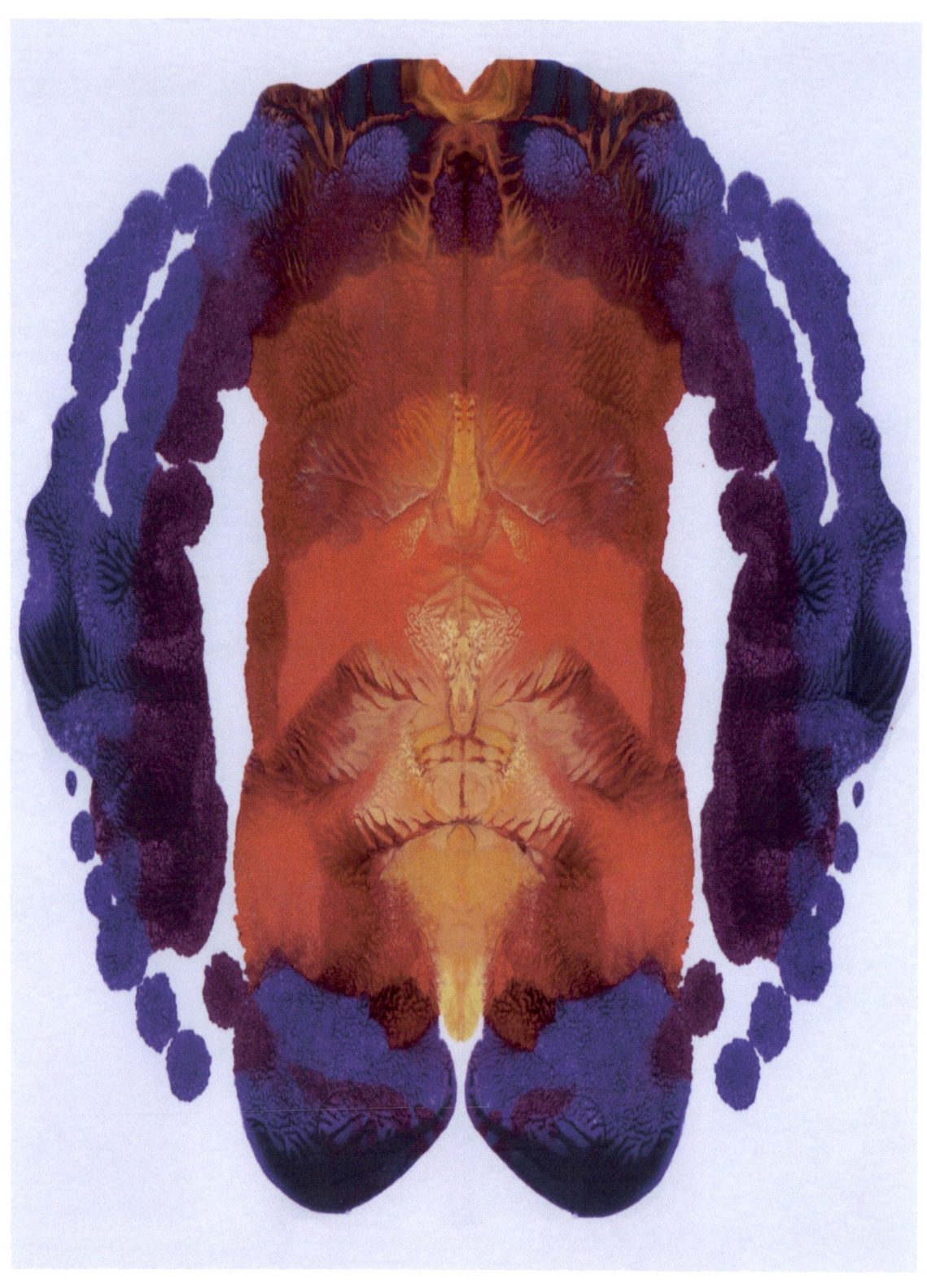

Image 38: A cat face, Capricorn, or ?

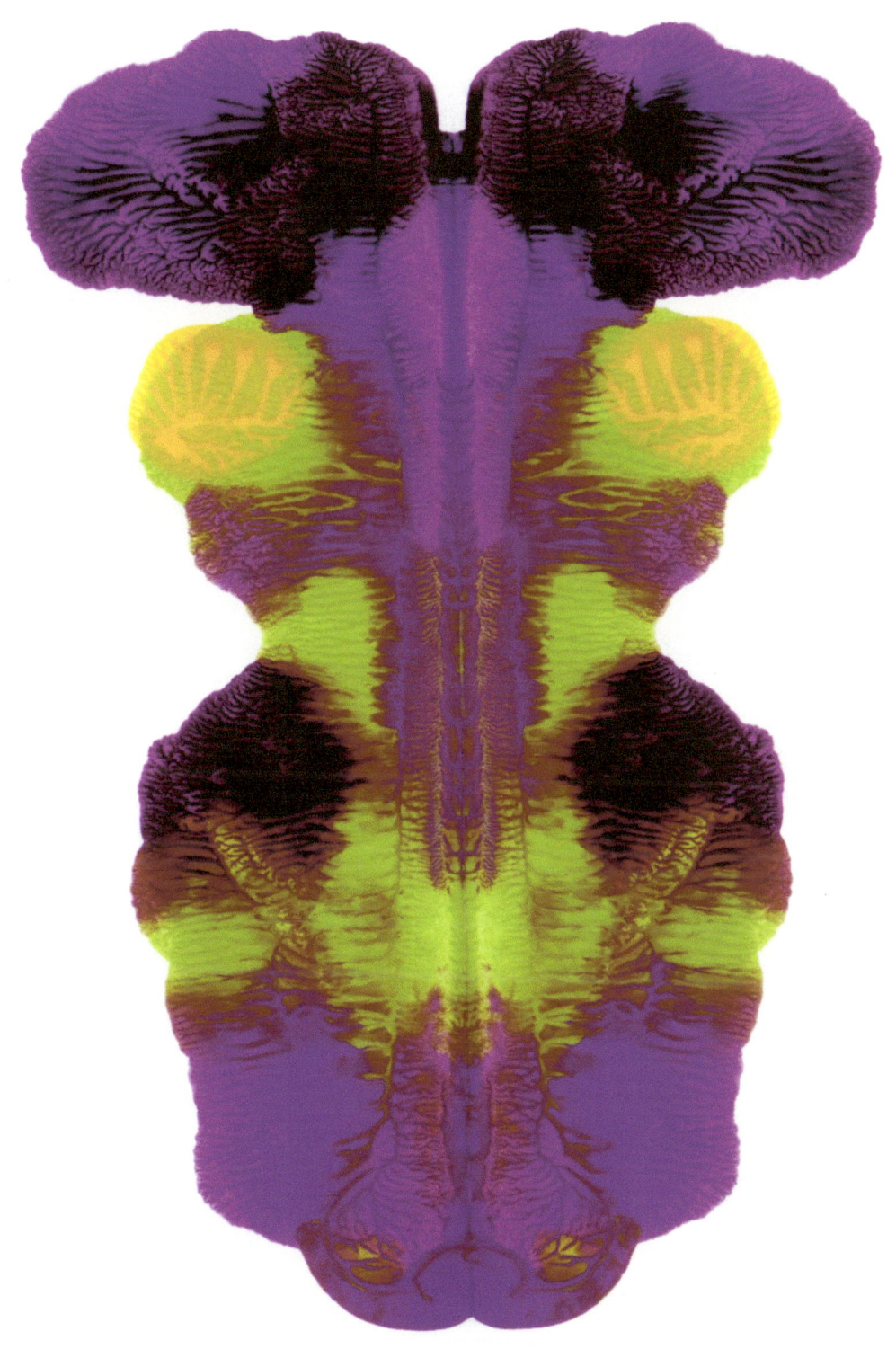

Image 39: A bird, plant, or ?

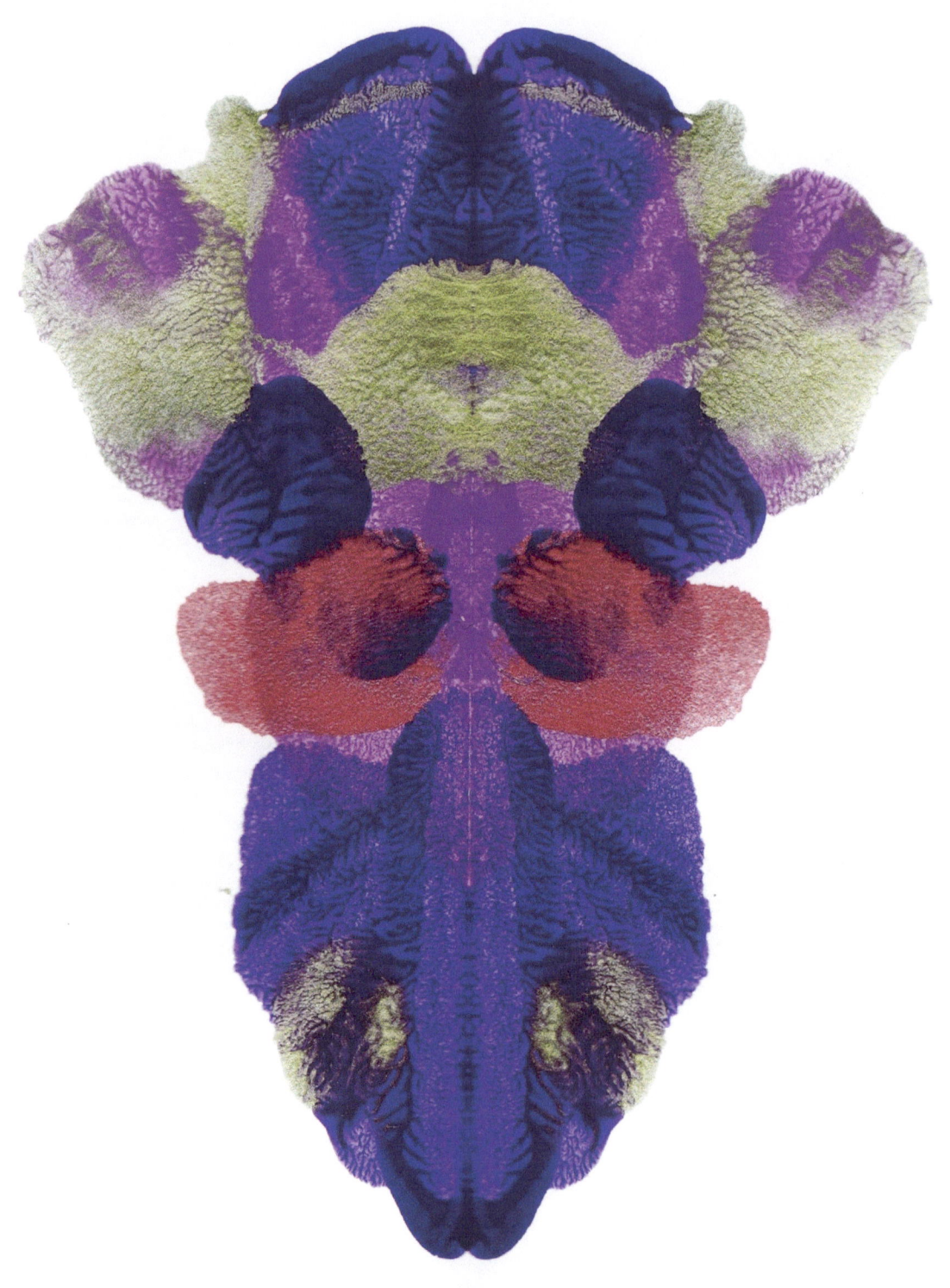

Image 40: A motorcycle, moth, or ?

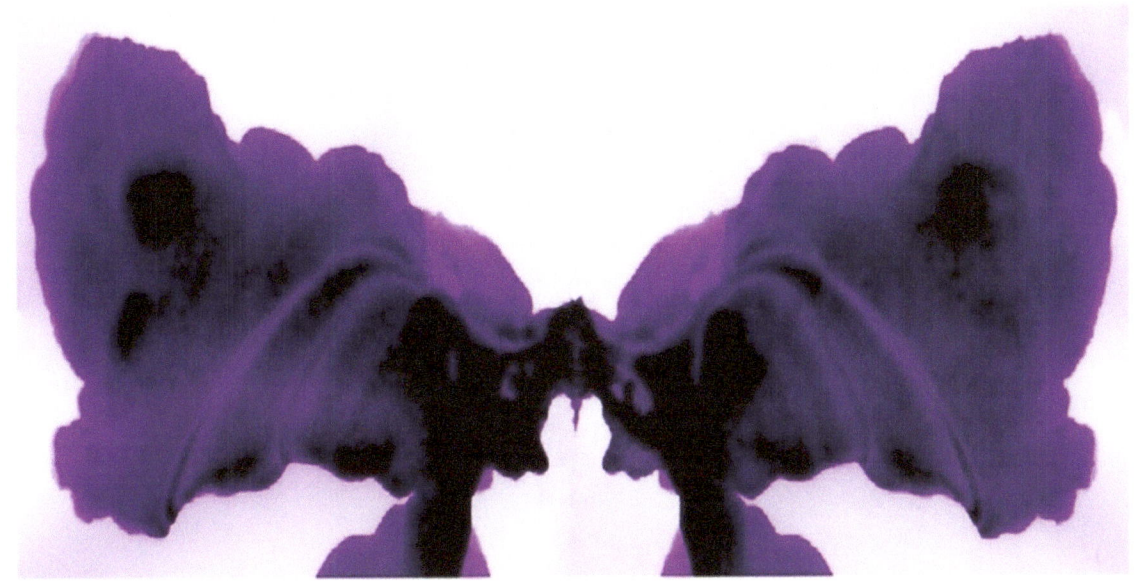

## In Case You Were Wondering About the Process...

When I started school in the 1960's, the first real writing implement we were allowed to use after the pencil was the fountain pen. Like many kids back then, I probably discovered how to make inkblot art by accident—spill some ink on a sheet of paper, fold it over, and voilà. Besides the anticipation of what might appear when I opened the paper, I liked the symmetry and ambiguity of the resulting images.

I haven't used a fountain pen in over fifty years, but I am making blots again. Now I do it with more purpose and sophistication. Instead of bottled ink, the images in this book started out as acrylic paint (like Image 40) or dye (the image above). Since the resulting sheets of paper ended up with pronounced folds and some wrinkles, I scanned them into a digital format. This also allowed me to adjust colours, proportions, etc.

Not all blots were worth keeping. Others turned out well enough that I find them interesting whichever end is up. If you have not already done so, turn the book upside down and go through it again. It's like having two books in one!

BK

www.ingramcontent.com/pod-product-compliance
Lightning Source LLC
Chambersburg PA
CBHW040415220526
45473CB00004B/1242